Improve Your Piano Playing

In the Right Way series:

The Right Way to Read Music
Begin Guitar

Improve Your Piano Playing

by

Dr John Meffen MA ARCM FTCL CERT ED

RIGHT WAY

Constable & Robinson Ltd
3 The Lanchesters
162 Fulham Palace Road
London W6 9ER
www.right-way.co.uk
www.constablerobinson.com

First published in the UK 2001

This edition published by Right Way, an imprint of
Constable & Robinson, 2008

Copyright © Dr John Meffen, 2001, 2008

A copy of the British Library Cataloguing in Publication
Data is available from the British Library

ISBN: 978-0-7160-2207-7

Printed and bound in the EU

Contents

Acknowledgements

It was the remark "what you are talking about is facilitation at the synapses", made by my friend and pupil the late Dr Mavis Taylor, which first set me thinking and reading about the workings of the mind, not just the working of the muscles, in connection with piano playing. This book is a direct result of that chance remark.

I am much indebted to Sir James Beament, who was for many years the Head of the Department of Applied Biology at the University of Cambridge, for reading various chapters of the book. His suggestions and advice helped clarify my thinking on many aspects, as well as bringing my information up to date.

My thanks to Mike Frankton who made such a professional job of setting the musical notation which appears at various points in the text.

Many thanks too, to my wife, Kathleen, who, though sorely neglected in favour of books, a piano, and a computer, still offered to draw the excellent illustrations which add so much to the text, and the pictures which bring a touch of humour to the book.

I would also like to express my thanks to Cassandra Birmingham the editor at Elliot Right Way Books who guided matters with a steady hand and made many helpful suggestions throughout the editorial process.

Finally, I would like to thank my many pupils who, over the years, have made me think of ways to keep the complications of piano playing in my mind while, hopefully, not implanting them in theirs.

End of Chapter Questions

Throughout this book, each chapter ends with a series of questions, the answers to which may be found by re-reading the chapter concerned.

Introduction

"The music teacher came twice a week to bridge the awful gap between Dorothy and Chopin." My task, not so daunting as that in George Ade's quip, is to bridge another awful musical gap. There are many books about music, musical history, musical appreciation (whatever that happens to be), harmony, counterpoint, musical forms and the like, and also many about piano technique, but explanations of exactly how these two aspects, general musical knowledge and specific information on how to play the piano, can be brought together are hard to find. It is this gap that I hope to fill.

There are many versions of the following anecdote; I give it in the way I first heard it. A young musician had travelled to London to attend a Promenade concert. Coming out of King's Cross station, somewhat bewildered by the number of people, and not knowing which way to go, he approached a gentleman whose face seemed to be familiar and asked "Can you tell me the best way to get to the Albert Hall?" The answer was unexpected, "Practise man, practise!" The familiar face had belonged to Louis Armstrong.

As musicians we are constantly told to "practise", this or "practise" that, not to forget to "practise" or not to skimp our "practice". But there is more musical dirty-work, sculduggery, and damage done in the name of "practice" than in any other musical pursuit. Everyone knows that it is necessary to practise – few know how to do it.

The essence of wasted practice time is crystallised in the much used admonition, "That was wrong – do it again." If something is wrong, the worst possible course of action is to "do it again". This implies the hope that, by some miracle, it will come right by itself next time. If it does, it is usually more by luck than management and the luck is unlikely to hold. If something is wrong, active and positive steps must immediately be taken to ensure that it is not wrong next time. If they are not, and the mistake is allowed to continue, it might, in the end, prove difficult, or even impossible, to eradicate. This is sad because with careful, but enjoyable, work it is possible, within the natural limits of every player, to acquire a sound and reliable technique.

My objective is to help anyone who wants to improve their piano playing. Since it is impossible to improve upon anything which does not already exist, I need to assume that the reader has at least some pianistic ability. That ability need not be great. The ways of working and thinking outlined in the following pages can be adapted to the needs of musicians of all stages, ages, and abilities. They are as appropriate for the beginner as for the serious student. They will also be helpful to parents with little musical knowledge who wish to help their children; they can, in fact, be of value to anyone wishing either to improve their own playing or to help others improve. Although specifically directed towards piano playing, many of the methods outlined can readily be adapted for use with other instruments.

Chapter 1:

Your Piano

An obvious opening to a study of how to improve your piano playing is to look at the piano itself, how it works, and what, from a player's point of view, makes it good or not so good. It will help you to understand more clearly what it is you are doing and aiming for, as well as how to achieve your goal of becoming a competent player, if you consider the attributes of the instrument on which you will be practising, and compare them with other pianos.

You probably have a piano already, but, if you do not, here are some things to bear in mind which will help your choice when buying one. It is always worth remembering that, however accomplished you are or you eventually become, you will only be capable of playing as well as your piano will allow. The following observations are mainly aimed at choosing an upright instrument, since they are the ones most likely to be found in the majority of homes, but many of the observations, particularly in reference to string lengths, apply to grand pianos too. After you have read them, and judged how well or badly your present piano measures up, you might even consider a change.

The tone of your piano is probably the most important factor to consider. There are many ways of judging piano tone, but since *you* will be using the instrument it is what suits you that counts. As well as tone there is

also the 'feel' of the action to consider, is it too heavy
or too light? Again, it is what suits you that matters.
The size and general appearance of an instrument can
also be important. How a piano will fit into your room
for size and style, as well as its musical qualities, can
influence your choice. And finally, do you wish to go
for a new or a used piano? In the end you must be the
judge of these things, but help can be given in making
your choice.

Whether you are buying old or new the best way to
come to a decision is to try many instruments, just
listening to one or two will not be sufficient. Your
local music shop is probably the best place to begin
because there should be a variety of instruments for
you to try. It is only by comparison that you will be
able to make a valid judgment, and it is much easier to
make comparisons if you can move quickly from one
instrument to another. It helps too if those comparisons are made in the same, or similar, surroundings.
The size and furnishings of a room can influence
sound considerably.

Tone Quality

Since it is so important, you should begin by assessing
tone quality. The sound a piano makes should be clear
and resonant; it should never be dull. It should not be
harsh, 'tinny', or strident, but it should not be too soft,
indistinct, or 'mushy'. Remember too that it will need
to suit the room in which you wish to play. If your
room has a thickly carpeted floor and lots of padded
furniture, the sound of the piano will be absorbed
much more than if your room has a hard floor and
mainly wood furniture.

Listen critically to the sounds of the lower and higher notes of the instrument. The lower notes can often sound indistinct and 'tubby', especially on small pianos. Such instruments, sometimes called console or studio size, vary from about three to four feet in height, whereas a full upright is from four feet upwards. Don't be misled by such terms as 'upright grand'. There is no such thing, even though some large uprights are sometimes called by that name. The confusion stems from the fact that at one time upright pianos had only two strings to most notes while grand pianos had three; therefore any instrument which had three was called a grand. Modern pianos do in fact have three strings to most notes, but only horizontal instruments should be called grands.

Instruments with greater string lengths will generally give better tone than those with shorter strings. Since the pitch of a note is determined by a combination of the length, tension, weight, and elasticity of the string, short strings need to be heavily weighted with copper wire to produce the lowest notes, whilst the very short strings which produce the highest notes must be held at great tension. Both of these factors affect the quality of sound of small upright and small grand pianos.

New or Second-hand?

A new instrument should be in excellent condition but if you are considering a used instrument you cannot rely on this being so. Beware of newspaper advertisements like the following:

'Piano for sale – cheap – suitable for beginner.'

The piano *might* be all right, but it is just as likely to be a worn out wreck only fit for the scrap heap. Buying a poor quality, or otherwise unsuitable instrument is a false economy. Good musical instruments are expensive, but they do hold their value. Pianos can suffer from many defects which can be at best costly and, at worst, impossible to rectify satisfactorily, but an instrument which is dusty, dirty, and out of tune might only need a little care and attention. It is well worth paying the fee of a good piano tuner if you are not sure: it could save you money in the end.

Inspecting the Piano for Yourself

There are, however, many things you could look out for before calling on expert help. An overstrung instrument, with underdamper action (these terms are explained as you read on) is best and these facts are easy to check. When assessing an upright, lift the lid on the top of the piano (the lid which covers the keys is known as the fall) and look inside. With an underdamper action all the piano hammers will be visible and the different thicknesses of felt on the face of each will be noticeable. However, if what appears to be a block of wood covers most of the hammers and only those to the right hand end of the instrument are visible, then the instrument has an overdamper action. Usually, the better pianos have underdamper actions, but, although I would advise you to go for one of these, not all pianos with overdamper actions are poor instruments. Underdamper actions are generally more positive in their reactions. The extra mechanism needed to place the dampers above the hammers in an overdamper action can cause noise and influence the touch of the piano. Having said this, many overdamper actions are quite serviceable.

While you have the lid up, check to see if the instrument is overstrung. Look at the tuning pins (known as wrest pins) which are just below the lid and to which the piano strings are attached. Near the left hand end there will be wrest pins, from which the strings run diagonally downwards towards the right. There will then be a gap before the next, and greater, set of wrest pins from which the strings run diagonally downwards towards the left. If this is the pattern you see, the instrument is overstrung, and it will be obvious that the strings do overlap. If there is no gap in the pattern of wrest pins, and the strings run vertically downwards with no overlap, the instrument is straight strung. There is a further possibility in that all the strings may run downwards slightly diagonally. This type of stringing is known as oblique, but again there is no overlapping of strings. Overstringing improves the sound quality and most new instruments will be made in this way. However, there are many older instruments on the market which are neither overstrung nor underdamped which could still be serviceable. Listen carefully to the tone quality of whatever instrument you are inspecting. If it does not match up with the description already given be wary of it and, if in doubt, consult a piano technician.

Key Action

The next consideration is the action of the keys; that is, how they respond to your touch. When you play on the instrument, none of the notes should fail to sound. If they do, further exploration is needed to find out why.

Sometimes the cause is simple and easily rectified, but this is not always so. Check that the keys go down easily, but that they do offer a certain amount of resistance to your touch. If they go down too easily or the dip (the distance the key travels before it hits the key bed) is very shallow, beware. Compare the resistance and the dip with a new piano if you can because a new instrument should give you the correct 'feel' for a standard touch and dip. If the used instrument you are trying does not give this 'feel,' or something very near it, and the keys appear to be loose and 'wobbly', get some advice before you buy. Play all the notes on the instrument from bottom to top and, while trying to play each note with equal loudness, listen very carefully. All the notes should speak evenly, none should be appreciably louder or softer than the others, always provided, of course, that you strike the keys with equal force. If there is inequality among them, advice should be sought.

The Pedals

Try the pedals (there should be two on most instruments, three on some) and find out if they work properly. This is quite easy to do if you know what to look and listen for. Lift the top lid of the piano again and, as you press the right (the 'loud', sustaining or damper) pedal, watch what happens to the dampers. These are small, felt faced blocks of various sizes which will be pressing on the strings. If the pedal is working correctly, they should all move away from the strings. With the pedal still depressed, play a few notes in different parts of the keyboard. All the notes you play should continue to sound, but they should all stop and the dampers should come back into contact with the strings when you release the pedal. Try this experiment a few times, selecting different notes each time; they should all continue to sound while the pedal is depressed and all stop when the pedal is released. If this does not happen, some adjustment will be necessary.

With the lid still raised, look inside the instrument while you depress the left pedal and you should see that all the hammers move forward, closer to the strings. Play a few notes and you will notice that it is more difficult to make a loud sound because the hammers have less distance to travel before they hit the strings. This is the better of the two usual types of soft pedal mechanism to be found on upright pianos. If the mechanism is of the poorer type, when you depress and release the soft pedal you will notice a piece of felt being lifted and lowered in front of the hammer heads. This is the 'muffler' type of soft pedal which, although it certainly makes the sound much softer, also kills the tone quality.

It is very unlikely that the instrument will be fitted with the best of all 'soft' pedal mechanisms, the *una corda* type. *Una corda* literally means one string. With this type of mechanism, depressing the pedal moves the whole of the keyboard slightly to the right so that the hammers strike only two of the three strings in the treble (upper) register, one of the two strings in the tenor (middle) register, and in all registers they strike the strings with the softer, less used portion of the hammer face, giving the sound a completely different timbre (quality). This is the type of soft pedal mechanism used on grand pianos and is much superior to either of the other mechanisms described, but is very seldom fitted to upright pianos. If a middle pedal is fitted to an upright piano it is often called a practice pedal. It is very similar to the 'muffler' type of soft pedal and is intended for use where a normal piano sound would cause considerable disturbance to other people. The middle pedal most often fitted to a grand piano is the sostenuto pedal, whose use is explained on page 110.

The Hammers

While the lid is still up you could check the face of the hammers which strike the strings. If the instrument has been frequently used, the strings will have cut into and compressed the felt on the face of the hammers. This sort of wear, together with excessive noise from the action, individual notes which are badly out of tune, broken or missing hammers, keys which have a lot of sideways movement, and anything about the mechanism which appears to be cracked or broken, are all matters which should be inspected by a piano tuner. Many of them might be easily and cheaply dealt with, but some may not, or may even be beyond repair. You would be well advised to find out before parting with your money.

The Importance of a Good Instrument

You might ask what this has to do with piano playing – a lot, is the short and accurate answer. An instrument that does not work properly or one with poor tone quality does not give you a chance to develop your technique. If the instrument on which you are practising has loose fitting keys and very shallow key dip, it will be very difficult for you to control your playing.

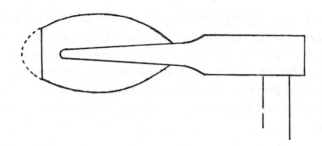

The diagram shows the end of a hammer whose felt has been cut off by wear. It will also be deeply cut by the strings. The dotted outline shows the shape the hammer should be. The felt covering on the hammers for high notes is very thin and could be cut through to the wood.

Notes which react to the slightest touch can inhibit the development of your technique. You ought to be able to feel the weight of the key beneath your finger and to control its movement accurately. On a well-regulated piano with standard touch and dip, as you press a key down very slowly you will, at about half its travel, feel a slight click. If you are controlling it fully, you ought to be able to continue the downward movement of the key past this point until it is stopped by the key bed. The click you felt occurs when the action passes the set-off at which point the hammer is thrown, forwards in uprights and upwards in grands, towards the string. If the speed of key descent is too slow the action will not set-off properly which means that the hammer will not be projected onto the string and there will be no sound. The speed at which the key passes the set-off point determines the loudness of the sound. It is therefore important that you have control of the key before the set-off point is reached, because, after it is passed, you can have no further influence on the sound until you release the key and depress it again. This is why it is critical that the combination of touch and dip of the key is as near standard as possible, and this must be the same for every key on the instrument otherwise you will find it extremely difficult to play evenly.

It is possible to become used to an instrument that is not working correctly and be unaware of the difference a better one could make. Always buy the best you can afford. At the time of purchase, look to its resale value. If you cannot buy the best, make sure you know the limitations of the instrument you are buying and aim to use it only so long as you must. An instrument with limitations can serve you well for a period of time, but you will become increasingly frustrated if you are capable of playing better than the instrument will allow. When a change is obviously necessary, a tuner, or a teacher, might be able to help. If you bought wisely in the first instance, a tuner's client or the pupil of a local teacher might be glad of the instrument you have.

The Piano Stool

It is not only the instrument which needs to be carefully chosen; do not forget about the chair or stool you will need to sit on. Piano stools should be of the right height. What that height is depends on you. The length of your arms, legs, and body will dictate the best working position for you. Most people prefer to adjust the stool height until their forearms can run parallel with the keys, or slope slightly down towards them, rather than have their elbows below key level and their forearms sloping upwards. But I have considerable reservations about being too pedantic over this. Anyone who has seen the famous pianist

Vladimir Horowitz in person or on the television will understand why. He held his hands in such a position that his wrists and elbows were well below key level, and there are many other pianists who do the same. More will be said about this in subsequent chapters, but what is most important is to keep the height of your stool constant. Using any chair which happens to be handy might not seem to have much bearing on how well you play, but continually trying to adjust to seats of different heights can affect your progress. An alteration to your seating puts the notes in a different position relative to your hands and arms and leads to uncertainty and inaccuracies. Take care to sit at the same height and in the same relative position to the keys every time you play – it will help a lot. Make sure, too, that the seat or stool is steady. A wobbly stool can be a curse. So too can those elegant, often Victorian, stools with a large metal or wood screw which makes their height adjustable. Many of these are very unstable. It is advantageous to have an adjustable stool, but do not trade stability for adjustability. The former is much more important. After all, you can always use a cushion.

Questions

1   *Why is it important to try as many instruments as you can?*
2   *Name as many attributes of good piano tone as you can.*
3   *Name as many types of poor piano tone as you can.*
4   *What effect will floor carpeting have on piano tone?*
5   *What effect will soft furnishings have on piano tone?*
6   *What effect will hard flooring have on piano tone?*
7   *What effect will wood furniture have on piano tone?*

Beware of the wobbly stool.

8   *Describe the sound of some small pianos.*
9   *Is there such an instrument as an upright grand?*
10   *Why are some instruments called upright grands?*
11   *What effect does string length have on piano tone?*
12   *What factors determine the pitch of a note?*
13   *What needs to be done to short strings to produce low pitched notes?*
14   *Why is it sensible to buy as good an instrument as you can?*

15   Is an old, dusty, dirty and out-of-tune piano always a poor buy?

16   How would you recognise an underdamper action?

17   How would you recognise an overdamper action?

18   Which of the two types is usually better, and why?

19   What name is given to the lid which covers the piano keys?

20   How would you be able to check if an instrument is overstrung?

21   What other types of stringing are there and how would you be able to recognise them?

22   What is the most usual type of stringing used on new instruments?

23   What is meant by the term 'dip' when discussing piano keys?

24   Why is it important?

25   Why is it important that piano keys are not too easy to depress?

26   What effect does the 'loud' pedal actually have on piano sound?

27   What are dampers and what do they do?

28   How can you check that the 'loud' pedal is working properly?

29   What kinds of mechanism can be worked by the 'soft' pedal?

30   Describe the 'muffler' type of soft pedal, and for what other purpose is a 'muffler' pedal used?

31   What does 'una corda' mean?

32   Name some of the things you need to check when buying a used piano.

33   How can a piano which is not working correctly prevent you from developing your playing?

34   What important considerations should be borne in mind when choosing the stool or chair that you use?

Chapter 2:

General Approach

In trying to improve your piano playing the focus of attention must be on practising. It is during practice sessions that we establish the habits on which we will rely in performance. Success in our playing depends on how good these habits are and how well they have been rehearsed.

It has been well said that amateurs practise until they get something right, but professionals practise until they can't get it wrong. Much time is spent practising. Most of it is directed towards acquiring the highest degree of muscular control of which we are capable. Much of the time and effort, however, is misspent. When we get something wrong, we often make some purely arbitrary decision about the cause and have another try to see if it comes right next time. It usually doesn't. The 'hit and hope' method rarely produces reliable results.

Since our brain controls all our actions, the reason why things go wrong must originally stem from the messages sent from it to the muscles which are to perform the necessary actions. These messages must convey to the respective muscles the exact information needed for them to respond and to produce the effect for which we are aiming. If things are going wrong, it is to the problems of internal communication that we must first turn our attention.

The hit and hope method seldom works.

The brain is a self-organising, pattern-recognising and pattern-using system. Exactly how it works in terms of electrical and chemical connections is not yet fully understood or explained, but a great deal is known about the effects of its working. Our nerve network is constantly active whenever we receive stimulation by way of any of our senses, but what actually happens depends to a large extent on our previous experience and knowledge.

To play any piece of music we must establish a continuous set of thoughts and actions on which we can rely; it is therefore imperative that from the outset our practice is not casual. An extra-musical example will help us to understand why. As I take a gentle stroll down a road, I may encounter many different smells. My previous experience of smells will tell me which are from a nearby rose garden, or a bakery, and which are from the drains. There might also be some others for which I have not as yet established any internal analysis pattern. These I could explore more fully, given the time and opportunity, but even slight exposure to them will have set in motion some exploratory action, however tentative, which could be helpful on some future occasion. However, a vague impression like this, based as it is on ill-researched information, might be decidedly unhelpful and, in the future, send me off in entirely the wrong direction if, on having gained an impression, I considered that I actually understood. This might be of no consequence, unless the vague impression led me to mistake an 'almondy' sort of smell as something to do with marzipan when it was in fact potassium cyanide.

When I attempt to play a new piece of music I will encounter some things I recognise and can account for and others for which as yet I have no well considered answer, just as I did on my stroll. My first priority will be to get my fingers to the right notes. The fingering patterns I choose could be influenced by suggestions on the copy, just as my recognition of a particular smell could have been influenced by a sign saying 'bakery'. If no external suggestions are offered, I will rely on my previous experience and knowledge of piano playing to choose a series of actions which will, often somewhat vaguely, be appropriate to my getting to the right notes. I might consider that I am just 'playing the piece through', or 'getting an idea of what it sounds like', or something of the sort, but whether I am aware of it or not, the learning process has begun. In this initial 'play through' a sequence of messages, which represents the performance, such as it is, of this piece, will have been sent from brain to fingers. Although it will not as yet have been clearly defined, a pattern of actions, sufficiently recognisable to follow wholly or in part on subsequent occasions, will have been established.

Some sections of it I might consider to be reasonably secure (smelling of rose gardens or bakeries), others might be less secure and not very comfortable (reminiscent of the less pleasant odour of drains). There will also be those which, though apparently comfortable, have their feeling of security slightly tinged with a certain vague apprehension (the 'almondy' smell not yet immediately recognisable as marzipan, but perhaps something like it).

Unless I take active steps to prevent it, further 'play throughs' will reinforce this pattern. Those parts smelling of rose gardens or bakeries I might accept as being known and reliable old friends, those reminiscent of the drains might be less pleasant but at least recognisable, while the 'almondy' smell could be a potential killer. The end result would be a hotchpotch of sketchily known bits, held together so loosely that they would readily give way under pressure. The patterns established by my 'play through' would no more ensure a reliable performance than my memory of the stroll would stand up to close questioning about whether the odour of baking came from bread, or some other type of baking, or the smell of roses came from Fragrant Cloud, Whisky Mac, or some other fragrant rose. I might be slightly more forthcoming about the drains, but a deep intake of the cyanide, mistakenly accepted as something else, could prove fatal.

It is unlikely that circumstances would arise in which I might need to subject the memory of my stroll to close and detailed scrutiny. My initial 'play through', on the other hand, would be put under such intense scrutiny every time I attempted to play my new piece again. Troubles must arise even with those aspects of the 'play through' which appear to be so well under control that they can be accepted as being known. They might be similar to other passages which I have played, but it is not safe to assume that they are exactly the same. Confusing 'like' with 'same as' is easily done, but the confusion soon leads to trouble. Future 'play throughs' will be insecure, contain many moments of doubt, and probably end in complete breakdown. Even if they do not, the seeds of disaster have been sown, and, unless appropriate corrective action is taken, the situation will only get worse.

Much of the trouble can be avoided if the initial approach to the music is well considered. Sensible preparation and careful work can discover the real danger areas and minimise their ill effects even if it does not completely eliminate them. Playing the piano bristles with so many complications that the stresses and strains of life, at least for a while, must take second place. Many people who learn to play do so for this reason and have no aspirations to become professional musicians. It is frequently argued on their behalf that they wish to play tuneful pieces and not saddle themselves with slow, boring work which might deaden their enthusiasm and turn them off music completely. To my mind, and to that of many people I have worked with, nothing can be more boring than making the same mistakes over and over again. This more than anything else is likely to kill enthusiasm and frustrate enjoyment.

Questions

1   *Why is practice so important?*
2   *Why must practice not be casual?*
3   *What is the 'hit and hope' method?*
4   *Why is the 'hit and hope' method seldom effective?*
5   *Why do we need to work on our internal communications?*
6   *What are the operating systems of the brain?*
7   *What are the inherent dangers of just playing a piece through?*
8   *Pianistically, what are the dangers of confusing 'like' with 'same as'?*
9   *What do you think are the differences in approach when practising something to get it right and practising it until you can't get it wrong?*

Chapter 3:

Methods of Preventing and Correcting Mistakes

If we leave matters to our self-organising system, it will devise some plan of action to solve whatever problem we are tackling, but it might not always be the best one. This solution will be stored and remembered, and the next time a similar situation or problem is encountered that pattern will be used. If we make frequent indiscriminate alterations, we will create many trackways which are recognised and stored ready for future use. But since the system, as well as being self-organising, is also pattern-recognising and pattern-using, we can never be sure which of the trackways will be selected on any particular occasion. In other words, unless we take great care we can create for ourselves innumerable possibilities for error.

To help prevent this situation from arising, or to make corrective moves if it does, there are some procedures that can be followed which it will be best to describe at the outset.

Inhibition

We are familiar with the term inhibition, used in the Freudian sense of frustration and repression; but by exponents of the Alexander technique it is used in an entirely different way. To C. F. Alexander, inhibition meant the ability to prevent an unwanted habitual response from taking place by deliberately creating a pause. Inhibition, in this sense, is of considerable use to us in improving our piano playing. The ability to exercise self-restraint by inhibiting an action, and thereby allowing us to think out the next move, is one to cultivate. It takes courage to decide not to have just one more 'go' to see if things 'come right' of their own accord. If we do have one more go, responsibility for that next move is thrown back onto our self-organising system, and if that has set us on the wrong track already it will be pure chance if things do 'come right'.

Thinking Time

Inhibiting an action in order to prevent making an error is an essential first step, but it is not an end in itself. It does, however, provide space to allow the next moves to be worked out. This space I call 'thinking time' and both its length and content depend on the particular circumstances. Knowing exactly when the concentrated thinking time should begin, and its detailed contents, will be discussed later.

Isolation

Isolating a section of a piece of music, working on it slowly and methodically, and then slotting it back into context, is a method frequently used by piano students for dealing with technical problems. It allows concentrated effort to be directed on specific difficulties without interruption to the flow of a musical work. But there are other types of isolation which have hidden dangers. There must be very few of us who can honestly say that we have never slowed down a difficult section of a piece and then continued as if nothing had happened. Isolation of this sort within the context of a piece can be effective, but only if it is carefully controlled. One of the dangers is that we can do it without realising, and by doing so we can build into the music rogue sections which do not match with the rest of the piece.

The prime consideration for most aspiring musicians is to play the right notes. Timing, rhythm, phrasing, tone, and style are all cast aside in the relentless search for the right notes. Playing a wrong note more than anything else will bring things to a halt, so our preventive methods must be directed towards this problem first. Speed is probably the most frequent reason for making mistakes, and it is in the early stage of our practice that it can be most damaging. I was fortunate enough to be taught by a pupil of Solomon (Cutner), the famous concert pianist. My teacher studied with him for a number of years and often recalled an answer he had once given her to a question about speed. On arriving for her lesson she frequently heard him practising but he played so slowly that it was necessary to listen for some time before she could recognise even well known works he might be studying. When she asked him why, he said that he often passed the Royal College where he could hear students playing scales at break neck speed, and hammering away at exercises, studies and even pieces at full gallop, but his direct reply to her question taught her more about practice than any lengthy explanation could have done. "At the College they are all practising for important things such as assessments, examinations, and even diplomas. But me,

I am just practising for the Albert Hall!" He had shown, precisely, the difference between the amateur and the professional in their attitude to practice.

These words from such an eminent pianist should make us take stock of our own procedures for learning the notes of any new piece. The proper use of inhibition and thinking time which will enable us to get the right finger to the right note are essential in the initial stages of learning. But, we must not forget that, when learning something new, the problem of fingering has also to be addressed. Settling on a sensible and workable fingering pattern in advance of concentrated practice of a new work is vital if mistakes are to be avoided. See Chapter 4 for more about fingering.

If we have worked out a sensible fingering pattern and we follow the procedures of inhibition, thinking time and isolation, particularly on those sections of a new piece which we can see are likely to give us trouble, we should never make any mistakes in notes. In reality, getting things right is not as simple as that. We are all certain to make mistakes, many of them, so the sooner we establish sensible and reliable correction procedures to use when things go wrong the better it will be. And we must not forget that, as well as the notes themselves, the note lengths, the rhythm (the two are not necessarily identical), the tone, the dynamics, the phrasing, and the many fine interpretative details necessary to play a piece well are all likely to go wrong at some time or other. The same general corrective procedures can be effectively adapted to deal with errors in all of these cases.

It would therefore make sense for me to outline how these procedures can be established and put into practice before we go any further. Mistakes are made before they are heard. This must be true since every action we make is governed by a conscious, or unconscious, decision to perform that action, at which point a message is transmitted to the appropriate muscles. The decision must therefore be made before the action is performed. It might be immediately before, or a little time before the action, but the important fact is that the decision-making process and the transmission of the message sent through the nerve network are both in advance of the action itself, whether or not we are aware of the fact. If the action resulted, for example, in a wrong note, it is useless to start the corrective process at the actual point at which the mistake is heard. The inhibition must take place before the moment of decision, to prevent the wrong message being sent, and to create a sufficient period of thinking time to allow a correct message to be substituted.

To begin the corrective process:

1   Select a piece in which you almost invariably make an error in notes at a particular point.
2   Start playing a few bars before this point.
3   Move slowly towards the point of error, taking one note or chord at a time and allowing a short period of thinking time between each move.
4   In each period of thinking time tell yourself:
     (a) Which notes you are going to play;
     (b) Which fingers you are going to use to play them;
     (c) How long each note or chord is going to be;
     (d) How loud each note or chord will be.
5   Exert pressure on yourself to keep the relative rhythms correct even at this slow speed.
6   Resist any temptation to give yourself a little extra

time to check what you are going to do or what
you have already done.

7   Above all, do not simply try to avoid the mistake.
     That is negative thinking. What you need to do is
     think positively about what is necessary for you to
     play the notes correctly.

8   As you approach the error, be aware of any feeling
     of doubt or confusion which will tell you that you
     are near the point at which the mistaken decision
     is, or will be, made.

9   Force yourself to continue beyond this point until
     you reach the note or chord at which the error is
     usually made.

10   Stop at the actual note or chord which is usually
     wrong, hold down the notes you are playing,
     whether they are right or wrong, and check exactly
     what it is you have played.

If the notes are correct, do not assume that you have
solved the problem because, as I explained earlier,
faulty practice will have created many trackways from
which your brain can select. The fact that on this
occasion the correct one has been selected means little
or nothing beyond the fact that a correct trackway
does exist, if only you can select it every time.

Repeat the sequence from step 2 to step 10 a few
times, reducing the thinking time between each step.
Each time you reach step 10 check the notes you are
playing and remember what errors occur. They could
vary on each occasion. Continue repeating the step 2 to
step 10 sequence while reducing thinking time until:

(a) You are brought to a sudden halt at one of the
     moves because you do not know where to go next; or

(b) You become aware that your next move will produce an error; or

(c) You find yourself actually playing notes you did not intend to play.

By reducing the thinking time, you are putting your self-organising system on trial. If its initial premise was faulty, applying pressure to it will make whatever fault there was become apparent.

Having found exactly where the wrong decision was made, your efforts must now be concentrated on substituting the correct message at this point so that the step–by–step sequence can bring you accurately to the correct note or chord.

To do this, the next task is to find out precisely what was wrong with the instructions in the original message. There could be many possible reasons, some of the most likely are listed below.

1   Were you attempting to use a wrong finger?

2   Was your hand turned at such an angle that you could not use the correct finger even though you intended to?

3   Were you using the finger you actually wanted for the next note?

4   Was your hand too far forward on the keys, forcing you to lift a finger over a black note and therefore making it difficult to place it cleanly on the white note in the narrow space between two black notes?

5   Was your hand too far back on the keys making it difficult for you to reach a particular black note?

6   Did your fingering for the preceding passage mean that the finger you wanted was, for some reason or other, not available?

7   Had you misread that particular note when you first began to learn the piece, forcing you to decide on each subsequent playing what the note was; the reduction in thinking time making it impossible for you to change your mind at this point, so making the error inevitable?

8   Was it for some reason that I have not mentioned but is now clear to you?

This might seem a long and complicated process, but when you become used to it you will be able to locate where the wrong decision was made, and what it actually was, in a matter of seconds. Like everything else, this method of working needs practice, but learning to use it is time well spent and it will eventually save you time and frustration.

It is absolutely vital that you find the real fault because attempting to substitute an alternative sequence of messages without detecting it is unlikely to prove satisfactory. Decreasing the amount of thinking time will eventually force you into making the error; a necessity if you are to eradicate it. I repeat yet again, do not be surprised if you produce a few different errors at this point since several patterns sending a variety of messages to hand and fingers may be available. You need to eliminate each of them leaving only the correct one, and you know you have done so when you have removed all feelings of apprehension or doubt. A little careful observation will enable you to recognise exactly what the error is and what is causing it. It often happens when you actually get the notes right that you are making an involuntary finger movement immediately before the potential error and correcting yourself before you play the right note. Check for such involuntary actions and try to follow the direction in which they are pointing; they could tell you precisely what and where the mistake is. Involuntary actions of this sort are mistakes waiting to be made. It is not always easy for you to detect these yourself. If you slow down you are less likely to make that involuntary action, having given yourself enough thinking time to avoid it; if you do not slow down, things might be moving too quickly for you to detect exactly what is happening. Someone sitting beside you can often help. If you direct their attention correctly, they might be able to see that slight tell-tale movement of a finger setting out in the wrong direction and then being immediately corrected. A friend willing to do this is invaluable.

To give a simple instance, if the mistake was a B natural being played instead of a B flat, sitting beside a student I can often see that in approaching the B flat the student's fingers are too close to the edge of the white keys when ideally they should be much nearer to the black keys. As the B flat approaches I can see a slight finger movement towards the B natural being made, and then the finger being hurriedly extended to try to reach the flat. Sometimes it does so, sometimes it doesn't. Seeing this happening I can advise that, at a particular point, the student's hand be moved further forward, making it easy to play the B flat and much more difficult to play the B natural, and mark this point on the copy as a reminder. This is just one particular example among many I could have cited. A friend who has no knowledge of piano playing might not be able suggest a solution to the problem in the way that I was able to do, but could at least tell you where you appeared to be making an unnecessary movement and what that movement was. Armed with that information, you will then be able to work out the solution for yourself.

I cannot stress too strongly the necessity of finding out precisely the nature of the error. It is tempting to try to save time by simply working out a new procedure. If you do this the old error is still there. Your new procedure might help you bypass it, but will not have eradicated it. Your old error is still lurking, waiting to catch you unawares, usually at some particularly important time. It is only when you know the exact nature of the error, and the precise moment at which the message containing the instructions which caused it was sent out, that you can successfully inhibit the faulty action and positively substitute a correct one in its place.

Having uncovered the true cause of the fault, do not expect that substituting the correct message at the correct time on one occasion will put matters right. It won't. You will no doubt have practised the wrong sequence of actions many times which means that it will have been established very firmly in your nerve network. You will need to approach this danger point with extreme caution for some time, making sure that on every occasion from then on you put the right pattern in place at precisely the right moment. Every time you get it wrong you are reinforcing the faulty pattern and thereby increasing the number of times you will need to get it right before the error can be removed.

The most effective method of substituting the correct pattern is to isolate the section within the context of the piece. Having established exactly what the error is, *deliberately* slow down the section in which it occurs in subsequent practice sessions, making the slowing considerable enough to give you time to think. This allows you to put the correct pattern in place each time and makes a sufficient enough difference in speed for you to notice that you are slowing down. It is important to make the slowing down considerable. If it is only slight, you can begin to accept it as the way you wish to play the section. This was the reason for my earlier comment about haphazardly slowing down to avoid a mistake. If the slowing is done consciously and deliberately it leaves a mark in proceedings which you will remember even when you have put the section back into context at the correct speed. Isolating like this has the added advantage that you will approach and quit the danger area using the same fingering pattern on each occasion. Isolating a section out of context can result in an inappropriate fingering pattern being used unless a careful check is made to see that the fingerings which approach and follow on from the section are compatible with those which begin and end the isolated section. If they are not, you will find that you cannot start the section on the finger you wish, and you cannot move back into context on the correct finger; in other words, by trying to remove one error you have created the possibility of two others. Carefully controlled isolation within the context can prevent this from happening.

Questions

1   *What happens if we leave matters to our self-organising system?*
2   *Why is it detrimental to make frequent, indiscriminate alterations to the patterns created by our self-organising system?*
3   *What is meant by 'inhibition'?*
4   *What is 'thinking time'?*
5   *What are the benefits and dangers of 'isolation'?*

6   What is the most frequent reason for making mistakes, and why is it most damaging in the early stages of practice?

7   What is the most vital step to take before beginning to learn a new piece?

8   Why is it useless to start the corrective process at the actual point where a mistake is heard?

9   List the steps for finding out where, consciously or unconsciously, the decision to make a mistake was made.

10   Why is it necessary continually to reduce the thinking time when trying to find the exact point where the wrong decision was made?

11   How would you go about finding out what was wrong with the original message which contained the mistake?

12   Why is it vital to find out the real cause of the fault?

13   Why should you not be surprised to find not just one, but a few different errors at that point?

14   What hints can involuntary finger movements give you to getting rid of errors?

15   Why is it difficult to detect involuntary actions if you slow down?

16   Why is it dangerous to substitute a new procedure if you have not found and eradicated the cause of the mistake?

17   Why is it being too optimistic to expect that, having found the cause of the error and substituted a correct procedure, the problem is solved?

18   Having substituted a new procedure, why is it important to take care that you put it in place every time?

19   What is the most effective method of substituting the correct pattern of actions?

20   Give some reasons why it is the most effective method.

Chapter 4:

Fingering

C.P.E. Bach, in his *Essay on the True Art of Playing Keyboard Instruments*, points out that more can be lost because of poor fingering than can be compensated for by artistry.

What was true in 1753, when the *Essay* was published, remains equally true today. The most basic element of all good piano playing is 'appropriate' fingering. The word 'appropriate' is better than 'correct' because, although there are many wrong ways to finger any given passage, there is seldom any single correct way.

Much depends on the size, shape, and agility of the hand of the performer, as well as on his or her mental ability to control and remember the number and the sequence of movements, which must run into thousands, required to play any piece of music. The information needed to reproduce these movements in the correct sequence has to be stored in our brain and made available for immediate use. A clearly defined fingering pattern is therefore essential for accuracy of recall.

An appropriate system of fingering:

1   Must suit the hand of whoever is going to use it;
2   Must allow the music to be phrased as the composer directs;
3   Must make it possible to achieve the dynamic range (from *fff* to *ppp*) required by the music;

4   Must allow smooth and accurate movement to be accomplished;

5   Should be as simple and memorable as is possible, whilst allowing for the requirements previously mentioned.

Having settled on an appropriate system, it should be followed every time the piece is played. This principle is obviously necessary in the difficult sections, but it should be observed in the simplest passages too. The latter are often under-rehearsed and played with any fingering which comes to mind because they are 'easy'. This is very short-sighted policy. Not only are the passages themselves sketchily known, but those which follow them are likely to be approached in a different fashion each time, resulting in the fingering of their opening notes being a hit-and-miss affair. This has at best an unsettling effect and at worst can create a permanent accident black-spot.

Establishing what the appropriate fingering system should be is the first essential. It is impossible to give a formula which will cover all eventualities, but it is possible to give sensible guide lines.

Even if you cannot play them fluently, you should know, or at least have access to, the conventional fingerings for all scales and arpeggios. There are many occasions on which a fingering pattern from a particular scale or arpeggio can be helpful, even though the piece you are playing is not in that key. If you do not know them, or have access to them, buy a manual of scales and arpeggios. There are many on the market. This will give you a firm foundation from which to work, as well as one from which to deviate in a consistent manner. This last comment is particularly important. Conventional fingering patterns will often suffice, but there are many occasions, depending on the context of the music you are playing, in which they will not. Sensible adaptations to fingering patterns are often necessary for the first, or the last, few notes of a passage in order to make it fit neatly into the flow of what has preceded it or what follows it. Adaptations to conventional patterns can only be made if the conventional fingering itself is already familiar to you. More will be said about adaptations in subsequent paragraphs, but a timely warning must be given now before troubles build up. You should mark very clearly any adaptation to conventional fingering patterns. The availability of a pencil and rubber is as necessary to a piano player when practising as it is to an orchestral player attending a rehearsal. It is part of an orchestral player's training never to go to any rehearsal unless equipped with pencil and rubber; it should be part of any piano player's training that no preparation for a practice session is complete without a pencil and rubber being immediately to hand. It is not sufficient to have them in the next room, because the likelihood is that there is where they will stay. It is dangerous practice to convince yourself that you will easily remember what adaptations you have made without the chore of writing them down – you won't.

Competent pianists ought to be able to work out fingerings for themselves. Having said that, however, it is always sensible either to use the fingerings marked on a copy, or at least to give them a fair trial. If they do not prove to be satisfactory, alter them as little as possible. An editor will have spent a long time working out a fingering pattern, so it would be foolish to ignore it completely. Although this advice holds good as a general rule, there are occasions when given fingerings can be altered to advantage.

Hands differ. They differ in size, in finger lengths, in extent of reach, and in finger widths. Long fingers can be helpful, but they can have drawbacks in matters of neatness in articulation. Hands capable of making extensive reaches can have certain advantages (Liszt is reputed to have had the ability to stretch an octave and a half) but adjustments might have to be made in fingering when they are required to execute lengthy passages in which the notes are close together. Wide fingers can be a curse, but on the hands of a master of the keyboard they appear to present little difficulty. Denis Matthews, a fine performer of Mozart's piano music, showed me a difficulty he had had to battle with throughout his career. His fingers were so broad that they could easily jam between adjacent black notes, yet his playing was noted for its neatness and and clarity of articulation.

Because of the many variations which exist between people, it is not possible for an editor to devise fingering patterns which will fit the hands of everyone wishing to perform a particular piece. If, for any reason, it becomes necessary for you to alter the given fingering, blot it out on your copy and substitute your own. Once you have made an alteration and find that it works, stick to it. Leaving any trace of a fingering you do not intend to use can be misleading. Your eye can catch a glimpse of a 4 or a 3 or whatever, with the result that you play the note with that finger before you have time to remember you don't want to do that. It is easy enough to get things wrong without inviting disaster, so make sure your alterations are clear, firm and, where necessary, LARGE.

Starting from scratch to devise a fingering pattern, or making alterations to an existing one, involves the adoption of certain general principles. Always keep it simple. The purpose of well thought-out fingering is to put your hand in such a position that you can make the next necessary move easily and safely. The most comfortable position for your hand is usually the normal five-finger five-note position; that is, keeping your fingers over a group of five notes and using the appropriate finger for any of the notes you wish to play. It is easy to turn this into seven notes, without alteration of hand position, by extending thumb and little finger by one note. It makes sense, therefore, to use your hand in the normal five-finger five-note position whenever you can and to move your hand up or down the keyboard keeping to that position.

Chopin always insisted on this from his pupils. He considered that the normal position for the right hand was to place the fingers over the notes E, F sharp, G sharp, A sharp, and B, and that for the left hand it was F, G flat, A flat, B flat, C. All his teaching work in

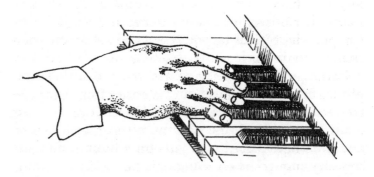

Chopin always insisted upon the five-finger five-note position.

fingering and in tone production began with hands in these positions. He taught his students to practise scales staccato at first, and advised wrist staccato (the technique for this is explained in Chapter 5) as a means for counteracting heaviness. The student's hand was to be held over the keys in such a way that the teacher's hand, placed under the student's wrist, felt scarcely any pressure. You can easily check your own wrist movement by doing this.

Chopin's next stage was a heavy staccato with fingers staying longer on the keys. The heavy staccato (see page 69) was then changed into what he called an accented legato (legato technique is also explained in Chapter 5) by obliterating the gaps between notes. This in turn was changed into a legato in which the fingers are raised considerably above the keys. The final stage was a legato performed with the dynamics ranging from *ff* (very loud) to *pp* (very soft), and speeds ranging from *andante* (a walking pace) to *prestissimo* (very quick).

Standard fingerings for scales and arpeggios form a strong, safe, and memorable basis. They also embody one of the most important general principles for moving your hand to the position required for the next notes: that of passing thumb under and fingers over. Chopin advised that fingers should be held high when training to do so.

Passing the thumb under is most easily accomplished if the preceding finger is on a black note. The converse is equally true; passing fingers over is most easily accomplished when the thumb is on a white note and the finger placed over falls on a black note. This suggestion seems obvious enough, but many occasions arise when we put fingers over, white to white, when a small adjustment to the fingering pattern could enable us to use the white to black, or black to white, principle. For instance, a left hand melodic pattern based on the scale of D major is more easily played by using 4th finger on F sharp and 3rd finger on C sharp, than by using the conventional left hand D major fingering of 4th finger on E and 3rd finger on B. The conventional right hand pattern of 3rd finger on F sharp and 4th finger on C sharp already uses the white to black and black to white principle when crossing fingers and thumbs, and is therefore the most satisfactory way of playing a right hand D major scalic pattern.

The black to white, and white to black, principle for thumb under or finger over movements, is very useful. It is always worth trying 4th finger B flat in right hand, and 4th finger F sharp in left hand in most major scalic passages, but, where that fails, the general black to white and white to black principle still holds good.

Finger crossing, a variation of the thumb under and finger over movements, is a useful skill to acquire, and was much favoured by eighteenth century theorists and practitioners writing about keyboard technique. It was also taught by Chopin, particularly for playing accompaniments in which there were wide intervals between notes.

Finger crossing can allow you to extend a pattern by a note or two without making a deliberate shift of hand and arm position. For instance, if a right hand passage ascends to the little finger and there is still one note to play before the passage descends again, it is often much simpler to play the odd note by passing the 3rd or 4th finger over the 5th, particularly if the odd note that the 3rd or 4th finger is to play is black. Similarly, if a descending right hand scalic passage begins on a black note followed by a white note, it can be helpful to start with finger 4 followed by 5, rather than with 5 followed by 4. This has the advantage of keeping your hand in the same position relative to the keys; fingering it 5 followed by 4 usually means that your hand must be pushed forward to allow your shorter little finger to play the black note and you are then left with the alternative of either pulling your hand back immediately, or, in many instances, of having to fit your 4th finger between two black notes — not always an easy movement to accomplish cleanly. Finger crossing can also help in extending the normal five-finger five-note position: by crossing a finger over the little finger it is possible to move your hand to a new position one note or more up or down without the necessity for any fingering complexities. This is particularly useful if the note to which you cross is black. These hints apply equally to your left hand.

Similar general principles to those used in scalic passages apply to fingering in arpeggio patterns. Thumb under or fingers over movements are most common, but such movements are probably better described as thumb under and along, or fingers over and along, meaning that in order to get your thumb or your fingers to the right notes you will need to make horizontal shifts of your arm in the direction you wish to go so that you can avoid ugly, and risky, turning movements of the hand or wrist. When performing thumb under or fingers over movements a little turning of hand or wrist is often inevitable, but for the sake of both accuracy and comfort, it should be kept to a minimum.

Consequently, it is not always good policy, simply by using methods of fingering, to attempt to gain a smooth, unbroken movement from note to note in arpeggio patterns. At a cinematic performance it is the speed at which the images are projected onto the screen that gives the semblance of unbroken continuity. In reality, as we all know, that continuity is obtained by the speed at which the images are being projected, deceiving our sense of sight. If the speed of projection were to fall we would perceive a set of staccato-like images.

So it is with playing arpeggios. If we can get the speed of the movement right we can deceive the ear into believing that the notes have been joined to each other, when in fact there is a small, but hopefully imperceptible, gap between them. Unfortunately it does not 'feel' legato when we are playing because we know there are gaps, but we need to judge the sound, not the 'feel'. It is much better to practise for speed and accuracy by making a horizontal shift of position, than to try to work out complications of fingering to bridge the gaps. This is not to say that a true pianistic legato cannot be achieved by fingering patterns, but clumsy or potentially hazardous movements should always be avoided. An explanation of how to obtain a pianistic legato is given in Chapter 5 under the heading *Weight Transfer Touch* (page 65).

When using the horizontal shift method, try placing your hand in position to play the first three or four notes of the arpeggio together as a chord. (The notes which form arpeggios in all keys will be shown in your book of scales and arpeggios.) Move your hand to the next group of notes, an octave up or down, and check how far you need to shift your arm to get your fingers from one position to the other. Go back to the original group and play the notes consecutively as an arpeggio, then move your arm up to the position you will need to play the next group. Do not worry at this stage if there is a gap in the arpeggio. The important things at first are to get the distance of the shift right, to avoid too much turning movement, to make sure that the correct finger falls cleanly onto its note, and to ensure that the speed of the horizontal movement of the arm is not used vertically to play the first note of the next group. If it is, each group will begin with an accent whether or not the music requires it. The gaps between the shift positions can be bridged as you become accustomed to the movement over the keys. Do this for each group of notes which form the complete arpeggio and rehearse the movement necessary to get your hand in the right place to play each group. Eventually try to get your arm to move smoothly and accurately to the right position, carrying your fingers to their positions above the required notes. This exercise should be practised each hand separately and with both hands together.

Leaps are best effected by the judicious use of lateral hand and arm movements, or of forearm rotary movement (forearm rotary movement is explained in Chapter 5, page 71), but they can be assisted by careful choice of fingering. It is difficult to give hard and fast rules because much depends on the size of the leap, and what happens immediately before and after it. Good performing editions will have fingering suggestions for such passages, and some also give alternatives too. You would do well to follow the fingerings given and make only such modifications as are absolutely necessary to accommodate the size of your hand.

Changing fingers on the same note without striking the note again can be a useful means of altering the hand position. This can easily be demonstrated by playing a note with your little finger, then by contracting your hand, substituting your thumb for your little finger without striking the note again. You can see that by that simple movement you have moved your hand a considerable distance across the keys without leaping. This is advantageous when playing legato passages, often avoiding over use of the sustaining pedal which might cause blurring of the harmonies. Like so many other useful techniques it needs to be carefully regulated so that it does not become habitual. Continual use of finger changing can interfere with the development of many sensible and reliable fingering patterns. The ability to creep about the keyboard by finger changing can inhibit bolder fingering sequences.

Changing fingers to facilitate fast, clean and precise repetitions of the same note is a useful skill to encourage. However, it became almost a fetish with editors of piano music in the late nineteenth and early twentieth centuries, and in many editions of Chopin's works, as well as those of other composers, a finger change is suggested every time the same note is repeated, regardless of whether such a change is necessary, or even easily practicable. Modern practice allows many more same-note same-finger patterns, but changing fingers for repeated notes can be helpful both from the point of view of clarity, and for the prevention of finger or hand fatigue.

Directional fingering also has advantages. When playing arpeggios it can be helpful to move outward from the centre of the keyboard using a 1–2–3–1–2–3 fingering pattern, but, when moving inward to the centre of the keyboard, to use a 4–2–1–4–2–1 pattern. Doing so helps to carry your hand further in the direction of travel than would be the case using 1–2–4 moving outward and 3–2–1 moving inward.

Avoid stretches involving finger 3 followed by 4, or 4 followed by 5, and their reverse. Stretching a minor third (i.e an interval of three semitones, such as D to F) might well be comfortable, but attempting the interval of a major third (i.e. an interval of four semitones, such as D to F sharp) or wider can be risky. Again, much depends on your own hand, but you might find your-self making mistakes in notes simply because you are using these pairs of fingers for stretches which they cannot easily accommodate.

Remember that your fingers are not all the same length. If you need to use your thumb (1st finger) or little (5th) finger on black notes you will find that moving your hand forward on the keys, and that mov-ing your hand back when these fingers are again needed on white notes, can facilitate playing. Fingering patterns which seem to be impossible become not only manageable but sensible when you use this simple forwards and backwards technique.

It is worth pointing out that some very old copies of piano music have what is known as English Fingering. In this system the thumb is indicated by + and the fingers then follow in order which makes the index finger number 1 and the little finger number 4. The fingering system now in common use in which the thumb is numbered as 1 is called Continental Fingering.

Try, as far as possible, to use the same fingering for each element of a sequence. A sequence is formed when a recognisable group of notes, usually making a melodic, harmonic or rhythmic pattern, is played a few times at different pitches. Melodically, for example, the notes D, F sharp, B, A, followed by G, B, E, D, followed by C sharp, E sharp, A sharp, G sharp form a sequence.

Forward and backward movement. Use the same fingering to play this short sequence. When your 3rd finger plays note D at the end of the second bar, push your hand forward so that your thumb falls easily on the C sharp at the beginning of the 3rd bar.

Sometimes, as is the case in this melodic sequence, the disposition of white and black notes in each of the repetitions is such that using the same fingering might not appear to be immediately obvious. Starting with thumb on D for the first pattern and thumb on G for the second is obvious enough, but starting with thumb on C sharp for the final pattern might not seem so obvious. However, bearing in mind the use of forward and backward hand movements described in a previous paragraph, it is possible, and indeed preferable, to leave the fingering pattern (1, 2, 4, 3) unaltered.

At the beginning of this chapter I listed five points to be borne in mind when working out fingering patterns, and to them I would add one further suggestion. The fingering adopted should also take into consideration the speed at which the music is to be played. Patterns which will work well at slow speeds might not always be suitable when played faster. It might, for instance, be safer at speed to use a lateral shift than to keep your hand and arm static and attempt thumb under, or fingers over, movements.

This chapter has been concerned with gaining fluency and continuity solely by fingering. In practice, the sustaining pedal, judiciously and discreetly used, can greatly help the fingers, but that is material for another chapter.

Questions

1   *Why is fingering so important?*
2   *Why is the word 'appropriate' better than 'correct' with reference to fingering patterns?*
3   *List some of the features of appropriate fingering patterns?*
4   *Why is it necessary to use the same fingering system on each occasion?*
5   *Why is it important to adopt this approach to simple as well as to difficult sections?*
6   *Give reasons for knowing, or having access to, conventional fingerings for all scales and arpeggios, even if you cannot play them all fluently.*
7   *For what reasons might it be appropriate to deviate from standard fingerings?*
8   *Why are a pencil and rubber important accessories to practice sessions?*
9   *Why is it sensible to give a fair trial to fingerings marked on your copy?*
10 *For what reasons might you consider making alterations to the given fingerings?*
11 *Having altered a fingering what must you always remember to do:*
    (a)   About its use?
    (b)   In connection with your copy?
12 *When devising or altering fingering patterns what things should you bear in mind?*
13 *What is meant by a normal five-note, five-finger position?*
14 *What are its advantages?*

15   *What is one of the most important general principles for moving your hand position?*

16   *What is the white to black, and black to white principle?*

17   *What is meant by the term 'finger crossing'?*

18   *Why do you need a horizontal shift when playing arpeggios?*

19   *How might you train yourself to use the horizontal shift when playing arpeggios? What was Chopin's advice?*

20   *Why would you not worry about a small gap in the continuity of your arpeggio playing at first?*

21   *How, and why, can changing fingers on the same note be useful in altering your hand position?*

22   *What are its other advantages and its dangers?*

23   *Explain the purpose of directional fingering.*

24   *Why should you take care over stretches involving finger 3 followed by finger 4, and finger 4 followed by finger 5?*

25   *What is meant by the term sequence and why is it advisable to use the same fingering for each element of it?*

26   *As well as the five points listed at the beginning of Chapter 4, what other factor needs to be considered?*

Chapter 5:

Touch

Piano touch is a highly contentious subject. There are many different ideas on how a key should be 'struck', 'depressed', 'addressed', or whatever term you might like to use for moving it the 1cm or ⅜" from its position of rest to the key bed.

Whilst it is not essential to know a great deal about the mechanics of your piano, a certain amount of information is valuable. Unless you know what you are doing, it is unwise to start making adjustments to the instrument itself, but from a performance point of view it does help to know what is actually happening inside the piano when you press a key or use a pedal. The information given in Chapter 1 was concerned mainly with assessing an instrument before buying it, but when discussing touch, that information, though similar, needs to be directed differently.

Key dip is an important factor when considering touch. The standard dip is about 1cm or ⅜". If, on your piano, it is greater than that, you will find it heavy and therefore tiring to play, particularly at speed. This will restrict your technique, and could even convince you that you are unable to play at speed. If the dip is less, although it will be lighter, and easier to play quickly, you will have difficulty in controlling speed, dynamics, and tone. It is easy to see why a heavy touch can be something of a handicap, but it might not be quite so obvious why lightening the touch can also be detrimental. If your piano speaks too quickly and easily, being continually under pressure to restrict your speed can become inhibiting and dangerous. Added to that, you will have less control over dynamics. You will find it more difficult to play softly and, as you will see in the next chapter, dynamics and tone control are very closely linked.

The 'tone' of your piano is governed by the quality of its manufacture and the skill of the manufacturer. You might find this bald statement of fact disconcerting, but it is nevertheless true. You may play the instrument in any way you wish, but you will not be able to alter its basic 'tone' quality. It cannot be denied, however, that some players can produce a much better 'sound' than can others from the same instrument. These two facts seem irreconcilable. The answer to this apparent dilemma must lie in what we mean by the word 'tone'. Since the tone quality of any instrument remains the same whoever plays it, the difference in 'sound' produced by one player as compared with another can only be accounted for by the manner in which each player uses that 'tone' quality which is common to both.

It is clear therefore that we can use the word tone to mean two entirely different things, and in doing so we are liable to become confused in our thinking about each of them, and, worse still, to confuse others when we talk about these two aspects as if they were one. About the tone of the instrument we can do nothing, we must accept it as it is; but we are in a very different position when considering how that tone is to be used. Here we have complete control, but it can only be exercised over note loudness and note length. Loudness depends on key speed, so our attention must be directed to the way in which we use our fingers, hands, and arms to impart the required speed at the right time. By listening intently to the sounds we produce we can make decisions about how well they convey the meaning of any piece of music we wish to play. But the listening process must do more than this; it must eventually also direct the actions we make to produce the sound. By this I mean that having a particular sound quality in mind can help our self-organising system to judge, before any action is made, how we are going to address the key.

This is all very well, but what must actually be done to accomplish these laudable ends? Some of the explanations about types of touch which follow may appear to be lengthy, but the processes themselves, once mastered, take little time to put into action.

Balanced Arm

The first step is to practise keeping your fingers, hands, and arms in a balanced state. Muscles can only pull, they cannot push, so equal sets of them are needed to enable arms, hands, and fingers to be moved in any direction. By a balanced state, I mean that in whatever position you hold your fingers, hand, and arm, your muscles should be exerting the minimum amount of force in opposition to each other to stop your limbs from collapsing. Try this experiment. Sitting away from the piano, in a chair without arms, rest your right forearm on your knee and relax it as completely as you can so that it rests quite heavily on your knee. Next, *without actually moving* (and that instruction is very important), think about raising your whole arm as if you were going to play the piano; then, still without actually moving your arm, let its own muscles take the weight of your arm. Your arm, even though it has not moved, should now feel lighter on your knee. Practise this a few times to get used to the feeling of only just supporting the weight of your arm without raising it. Try the same experiment with your left arm, and then try it both arms together. When you have become used to the feeling of a balanced arm you will have an immediate guide as to how tense your arm is. Without such a guide, it is difficult to assess the state of tension in your arms and hands. Too great an amount of tension and too great a degree of relaxation are both detrimental to movement, and your ability to assume the balanced state quickly and accurately will greatly enhance your fluency.

Having got used to the balanced feeling, raise your arms to a piano playing position, hold them there, and try to induce a similar feeling in your arms and hands as you had when they were resting on your knee. They will not feel quite so free because your muscles will be supporting the weight of your arms, but try to make them feel as free as you can. I hesitate to use the word relaxed in this context because a relaxed arm must fall and hang loosely by your side. Some tension is needed in your shoulder to hold your arm in the playing position, and also in your elbow and wrist joints to keep them from collapsing. Now move your forearms, hands, and fingers as if you were playing the piano, whilst trying to retain the feeling of freedom and balance you had when you first lifted your arms into a piano playing position. Still in the piano playing position apply just enough force to make your right arm reach out as if you were about to play a high note, stop the outward movement when your hand is above the imaginary note and let your arm, hand, and fingers assume the balanced feeling. Do this a few times, assuming the balanced state as soon as your hand has reached the position of the imaginary note. Do the same with your left arm, aiming for a low note, and then repeat the exercise with both arms together. The object of this exercise is to practise re-establishing the balanced state as quickly as possible after making a lateral arm movement. Any movement must be made with the minimum of effort, and you must be able to return to the balanced state immediately after that minimum effort has accomplished its task, in readiness for the next move.

Types of Pianistic Touch

Although some modern compositions require the keys to be struck with the palm of the hand, the fist, the forearm, or in some other fashion, the most usual way of contacting them is through our fingertips only. When we describe pianistic touch as hand or wrist touch, forearm touch, whole arm touch, or finger touch, we are referring to the source of the driving force which propels our finger into the key.

Finger Touch

In this type of touch we strike only with finger power, unassisted by any hand, wrist, or arm movement.

Hand or Wrist Touch

In this type, power to strike the key comes only from vertical movement of the hand at the wrist joint. The finger used to strike the note must stay firm enough to prevent it collapsing under pressure.

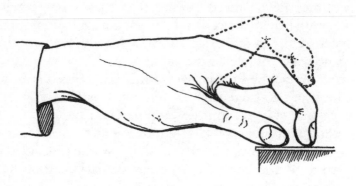

The action for pure finger touch, the movement coming from the knuckle joint only.

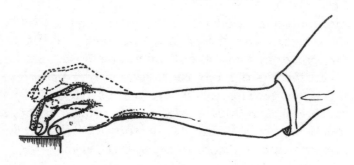

The action for pure hand or wrist touch, the movement coming from the wrist joint only.

Forearm Touch

The power to strike the key comes only from vertical movement of the forearm pivoting at the elbow. In this case both finger and hand stay firm. There are other forms of forearm touch, but they will be described later.

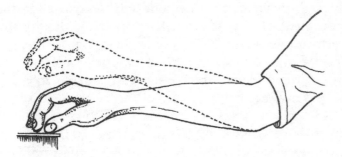

The action for pure forearm touch, the movement coming from the elbow joint only.

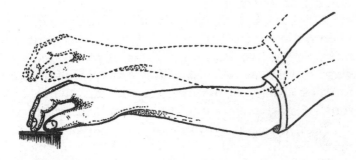

The action for pure whole arm touch, the movement coming from the shoulder joint only.

Whole Arm Touch

The power to strike the key comes only from vertical movement at the shoulder and all joints between shoulder and finger tip should remain firm.

These brief descriptions refer to what might be called 'pure' touches, meaning that the striking power comes through movement at one joint only, unassisted by the movement of any others. I have used the description 'vertical movement' in connection with hand, forearm, and whole arm touches to distinguish it from the lateral movements which need to be made to bring fingers over the correct notes.

Remember, when using each of these forms of touch, your arm should remain in the balanced state as much as possible. Only the minimum amount of tension needs to be used to perform each action, and after the movement of striking the key has been accomplished, your arm should again assume the balanced state as quickly as possible, whether or not you are holding down the note.

Except perhaps for finger touch, these touches are seldom used in their pure form. Finger movement will often be used to assist any forms of touch; hand or wrist movement will assist forearm and whole arm touches; and forearm movement will assist whole arm touch. Using touches in combination helps to prevent stiffness, as well as allowing for fine adjustments to be made to the speed at which the key is depressed, thereby controlling the volume of sound. Even if touches are not used in their pure form, it is important to be aware of the source of the main driving power at any moment. If, for instance, we are producing too great a volume of sound, we might choose to use a driving force controlled by less powerful muscles – hand instead of whole arm for example; but if this is not easily possible we might allow the controlled collapse of our wrist to absorb some of the power being imparted to the key, controlling its speed in that way.

The technique of controlled collapse at any particular joint is a useful and efficient method of ensuring fine control over volume. A slight bounce of the wrist joint can be compared to a slight bending of the knee joints to absorb some of the impact when jumping. With practice, a very slight bounce at the wrist can have a marked effect on volume, particularly of chords which need a fairly firm finger and hand position to ensure that all the notes sound together. Joints used in this fashion can be compared to spring steel – strong but flexible – instead of cast iron – strong but unrelenting.

Speaking in general terms, the larger the member being used, the greater the volume possible, because the larger the muscles the greater is the force available to impart speed to the key. Although it is not necessary for the larger muscles to be used only to create loud tone, they will be more cumbersome than smaller ones in the production of a soft tone.

Weight Transfer Touch

Legato playing is made more reliable by using what is usually called weight transfer touch, rather than by using the types of touch so far described. The following instructions will help you to create the right feeling in your fingers, hands, and arms for producing weight transfer touch.

Hold your right arm in the balanced state so that your middle finger is touching the G above middle C. Strike the note G and hold it down with the minimum of force. Now gradually relax your shoulder muscles which should so far have been gently supporting your arm, and let the weight of your arm bear down on the note G via your wrist, hand, and finger, making sure that your wrist and knuckle joints do not collapse under the weight. Do not physically push down on the key; rather, let your arm weight hang on the key, keeping your forearm, from knuckle joints through your wrist joint to your elbow, either horizontal or gently sloping down towards the key. Your upper arm and shoulder should feel quite relaxed, but you should feel that your finger is supporting a considerable weight. The knuckle joint of your middle finger could well be higher than the other knuckle joints because of the extra weight it has to support.

In order to check that everything is right, bring your arm back into the balanced state while keeping the note G depressed, thus reducing the weight on your finger. Next, let the weight bear down on your finger again, just by relaxing your shoulder muscles. Do this transfer many times, making little or no movement of your finger, hand, or arm, until you are sure that you can create the feeling of supporting your arm weight every time, without applying downward muscular force, that is, without pushing.

Still keeping your middle finger on note G, let your arm weight bear down on that finger again; then raise your index finger over the note F and strike the note F, transferring the weight of your arm onto your index finger, and at the same time lifting your middle finger from the note G. Your index finger, moving down towards the key bed, should be passing the set-off point (see page 19) for the note F just as your middle finger is about to leave the key bed of note G. Some teachers describe this as a see-saw movement of fingers, but, however you think of it, your fingers should pass each other almost on key bed level. When your index finger reaches the key bed and takes the weight of your arm, you will probably see that its knuckle joint is now higher than the others.

Now play the notes F, G, A, and B in turn by transferring your arm weight from note to note, watching the effect on your knuckle joints, and feeling the transfer of your arm weight from finger to finger. Your 4th finger has to work much harder than your index or 2nd fingers so as to support the weight and its knuckle joint may show more prominently than those of your other fingers – this might apply to your little finger too. Continue playing these four notes in any order, not always playing adjacent notes, making sure that the weight of your arm is transferred from finger to finger without any interruption. At no time should your arm assume the balanced state with your fingers at, or above, key level. Listen to each of the notes as you play them. There should be no break between the sounds and there should be no variation in the volume.

If you wish to make some of the notes louder than others, bring your finger down more quickly onto the key. You can also lighten your arm weight, bringing your arm closer to a balanced state, by allowing your shoulder muscles to take more of the weight of your arm. Alterations in the speed of the strike, and variations in the amount of arm weight brought to bear on the keys will produce different volumes of sound, but to keep your playing to an even legato, you will need to concentrate on keeping the transfer of arm weight, whatever weight that is, constant. After a little practice you should be able to play an excellent legato, with variations of volume as required, every time. Unless marked otherwise, legato playing is generally expected and, if the notes are joined by phrase or slur marks, legato is certainly expected.

Weight transfer touch is one of the most fundamental keyboard techniques. For practice purposes, at least until you become accomplished in using it, always apply considerable weight and keep the volume level high. By doing so you will be able to "feel" the weight transfer process more surely than you would if the arm weight is minimal. At first, it is practice in the transfer technique itself that is important; later you will find that you are unconsciously using it for all legato passages, regardless of their speed or volume. It is the upward reaction to the weight of your arm, felt in your fingers and hand, that will help you to keep your playing even. As you become familiar with the "feel" of weight in your fingers and knuckles, you will be able to detect it and make use of it, however light the weight you are applying might be.

Melodies consisting of next door notes, or notes within the stretch of your hand, can readily be played legato with weight transfer touch; but those which contain wide leaps present some difficulties. To be effective, weight transfer touch depends on your arm weight being continuously brought to bear on the keys, but this is not possible when you need to move your hand some distance laterally to effect a wide leap. Legato pedalling, described in Chapter 8, page 112, can help bridge the gap, but much can be achieved without use of the pedal if the length of time your hand is lifted off the keys is very short. Practise the technique of making the leap in the shortest possible time by holding down the note before the leap until it is virtually too late to get to the next note on time. At that point, leap to the next note as quickly as possible. This instruction seems obvious enough but there are dangers. The speed at which a key is depressed governs the volume of sound, therefore the speed of your lateral movement must not be used to strike the key to which you are moving. If it is, you will make an accent, and unless the music demands one at this point, an accent is the last thing you want when playing legato. To avoid this, the leap must be made quickly and accurately, and be very carefully controlled. At the end of the leap your finger must 'drop' into the key, not hit it. It is surprising how adept you can become at covering what must be a break in the weight transfer. You will generally be aiming to make the two notes which form the leap equal in volume, but this is not always necessary. They must fit with the general rise and fall of the phrase in which they occur, but it is easier to accommodate if a slight difference in volume is appropriate. Couple this skill with judicious use of legato pedalling (described on page 112) when necessary, and you will be able to make a very good legato sound in all circumstances.

Staccato Touch

Playing staccato needs a different approach. By placing a dot above or below a note, a composer or editor is indicating that a light staccato is required. The instruction 'staccato' refers only to the *end* of a note, not its *beginning*. By this I mean that, when light staccato is required, a note is simply quitted early, not struck more forcibly than its neighbours. Students often, in their eagerness to release a note early, actually hit it more strongly in the beginning. This happens simply because their thoughts are concentrated so much on applying enough power to lift their hand quickly from the note, that they run into the error of supplying that force a split second before it is needed, hence producing a short, but accented note. If a reinforced staccato (*staccatissimo*) is required, it will be marked with a triangular shaped dot above or below the note (see page 129). A light staccato note should be approached as if it is going to be played legato, but should be released fractionally before the written length directs, making a very short break between it and its neighbour, just enough "to let the light in". Performed in this way, a staccato quaver and a staccato crotchet will, as they should, be notes of different lengths. No one in legato playing would make a crotchet the same length as a quaver (or at least it is to be hoped that they wouldn't) but it is surprising how many students make a staccato crotchet as short as a staccato quaver.

Finger Staccato

Staccato is a style of playing rather than a specific form of touch, but its execution is governed by how we use our fingers and arms and so needs to be considered at this point. The lightest type of staccato, particularly when played at speed, is best done by finger touch only. Some authorities suggest a stroking action, drawing the finger across the key towards the palm of the hand, whilst others recommend a vertical lift of the finger. Both methods require a balanced arm and a delicate finger action.

Wrist, or Hand, Staccato

This is done by a lift of the hand using only the wrist joint. This type of staccato action is performed more easily if your forearm is held slightly above key level and your hand and fingers are allowed to point downwards towards the keys than it is if you keep your wrist low and raise your hand above wrist level. This is the type of staccato action Chopin advised his pupils to use to counteract heaviness in their playing (see page 47).

A staccatissimo note is played with an accent and is usually allowed to sound only for a short time, but even then a crotchet marked staccatissimo should be longer than a quaver similarly marked.

Non Legato

There is an intermediate stage between legato and staccato called non legato. This is a most useful effect in that it can add clarity without spoiling the general flow of the music. To attain a good non legato technique, first play the passage in question with a well controlled legato touch. When it is running smoothly and evenly, momentarily break the weight transfer feeling between each note by allowing the key you will be releasing to complete its upward travel just before the key you are depressing passes its set-off point. The break in the weight transfer feeling should not be as noticeable as in a staccato passage, but at the same time should be significant enough momentarily to separate the notes in question. The actual length of the notes, as well as the gaps between them, can only be judged by careful listening.

Forearm Rotation

Another technique which is of considerable use to all pianists is forearm rotation. Try this preliminary exercise away from the keyboard first. Sitting again in your chair without arms, raise your right hand to a playing position, close your fingers lightly to form a fist, and hold your arm in a balanced state. Rotate your fist clockwise, moving your forearm at your elbow only, until your fingers are showing uppermost, then rotate it anticlockwise until the back of your hand is uppermost. Do this a few times, keeping your upper arm still and rotating your forearm only. Try the same preliminary exercise with your left fist. Your arm should remain in the balanced state all the time with only the minimum amount of tension at your shoulder to support your arm, and the minimum amount of force in your forearm to perform the rotating movement. Do not allow your arm to stiffen; if it does, use less force.

Now sit at a piano keyboard, raise your right arm to a playing position, but on this occasion open your hand as if you were about to play. Keeping your arm in a balanced state, supported at your shoulder as before, place your thumb about an inch above middle C and your little finger a similar distance above the C an octave higher. Rotate your forearm anticlockwise firmly enough to make your thumb play the middle C while making sure that it does not give way under the impact. Now rotate your forearm clockwise, lifting your thumb off the middle C, and bringing your little finger down firmly enough on the upper C to make it play. As with your thumb do not let your little finger collapse on impact. The rotation should bring your thumb at least three or four inches above middle C. Now rotate your forearm anticlockwise again, bringing your thumb back down on middle C and lifting your little finger at least three to four inches above the upper C. Keep on rotating your forearm so that you play the C's alternately. Gently increase the speed of rotation until you are moving as fast as you can without stiffening. Altering the speed of movement into the key will increase and decrease the volume while rotating your forearm, but never allow your arm or your wrist to stiffen.

Try the same preliminary exercise with your left fist and forearm. Transfer it to the keyboard as you did with your right hand, using your thumb on middle C and your little finger on the C below. Again be careful not to allow any stiffness to creep into your arm or wrist.

Forearm rotation is a natural and fundamental arm movement needed for so many daily tasks that its use escapes notice. It is only when it is applied to a specific activity such as piano playing that the movement needs to be explained at all. Like weight transfer touch, forearm rotation is one of the basic elements of piano technique. Using it as I have described will produce a pianistic "roll", but this is only one of its many uses. My description also emphasised the rotary movement by suggesting that your thumb and little finger should alternately be raised high above the keys. I have done this to illustrate the nature of the movement and to encourage you to get used to the "feel" of it. In practice the rotation will most likely be small. In fact, to the onlooker it might easily be missed completely, but to the performer even the slightest amount of rotation can frequently assist many movements round the keyboard. Certain skips or leaps can be made easier by its use, and it can also help in increasing speed and volume when playing trills using any two fingers.

Like many useful techniques, however, forearm rotation can be over done. It is very easy to slip into the habit of playing notes by rotating your wrist rather than by striking them directly with your fingers. It is a technique in its own right, and a useful assistant to, but not a substitute for, other forms of touch.

Vibrato

Liszt, it has been said, played rapid octaves "as if he were shaking cards out of his sleeves". It is possible neither with normal finger movements, nor with vertical or rotational movement of the forearm or of the whole arm, to produce a visual effect such as this. It can only be done by forward and backward movements of the arm. The main element essential to this type of touch is a push-pull action by the upper arm, moving the forearm and hand forward and backward across the key. The hand and fingers must remain firm throughout to enable the full force of the action to be transmitted to the keys. This push-pull action is usually coupled with a rise and fall of the wrist which helps to avoid stiffness. Although the details of how this action is to be performed vary depending on who is describing it, the push-pull type action is common to all.

The 'push' action of vibrato, with the wrist parallel to the keys and hand pushed forward on the keys.

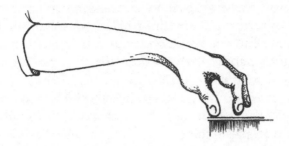

The 'pull' action of vibrato, with the wrist raised and hand drawn back towards the front edge of the keys.

Before using this technique at the keyboard, it is helpful to practise it on some suitable hard surface such as a table. Place your hand, in a playing position, on the table. Keeping your forearm and hand horizontal and parallel with the surface of the table, push your hand forward by moving your upper arm and allowing your elbow to bend to keep your forearm parallel to the table. Next, pull your forearm back again and let your wrist bend upwards slightly so that when you move your forearm forward again there will be a slight downward pressure as your wrist flattens out. Repeat this push and pull movement many times, keeping your arm as near to the balanced state as possible whilst doing so. This is a useful type of touch, particularly for playing rapid octaves and quick repetitions of chords.

Finally, a few general comments about touch should prove useful:

1   Stiffness should always to be avoided.
2   A moving joint cannot be stiff, so one of the best

ways to avoid stiffness is to move.

3   Keeping your arm in a balanced state will allow
     your fingers, hand, and arm to be ready for imme-
     diate action – if your arm is too relaxed, tension
     will need to be applied to it before you can move;
     if it is too tense, it will need to be relaxed before
     you can move. Either of these conditions will take
     up valuable time.

4   As far as possible, keep your fingers in line with
     the keys. By this I mean do not turn your hand too
     far to the right or to the left laterally across the
     keys, because by doing so you strike the keys from
     the side rather than from the top. Also, if the
     turning is severe enough it will cause stiffness in
     your wrist.

5   Remember the above suggestion (4) when you are
     performing thumb under and fingers over move-
     ments – do not turn your hand at the wrist joint
     very far to left or right.

6   If you are playing on black notes, particularly if
     you need to use your thumb or little finger, push
     your hand forward over the keys. Pull it back
     again when you resume playing mainly on white
     notes. This deliberate forward and backward
     movement can help you to hit the right notes, and
     to control the tone by striking the notes cleanly
     and accurately.

7   If an action feels clumsy, awkward, or difficult
     there is usually something wrong. Have a close
     look at:
     (a) Your fingering pattern;
     (b) The position of your hand;
     (c) The position of your arm.

8   Do not let the outside edges of your hands droop.

It is better to lift your little finger knuckle slightly. This will make the back of your hand fairly flat, rather than letting it fall away towards your little finger. If you don't do this, your little finger will not be in a good playing position and will tend to be moving sideways into the key rather than vertically onto it.

9   When leaping down to a single low note with your left hand, or up to a single high note with your right, strike that note with your little finger. Many students use their stronger third finger under these circumstances, but this makes the distance to leap greater, and it can put your hand out of position. Remember to play the note with the tip of your finger, do not play it with the side of your finger by using rotary movement.

10   When using hand touch, it is usually more effective to let your hand droop down slightly below wrist level rather than raise it up above wrist level. Try this experiment and you will soon understand why. Raise your right, or left, arm to the playing position. Hold it in the balanced state in such a way that a line from your knuckles to your elbow is parallel to the keys. Now raise your hand at the wrist joint. Very soon you will feel that your hand and wrist are stiffening. Instead, try holding your arm so that your hand droops down a little below wrist level. Now use your wrist to raise and lower your hand. You will find that there is greater movement available to you before your wrist and hand become stiff.

I have tried to describe some of the most basic forms of piano touch. You will probably find that you use them in combination rather than in their pure states. Which form of touch you will need at any particular time is something you will eventually need to come to terms with for yourself. Generally, the best advice I can give is to use the smallest forces you need to do the job. By that I mean do not use whole arm touch where finger touch is all that you need. Save your whole arm movements for strong, loud passages; they will be more cumbersome than finger or hand movements, but they will tire less quickly. Use finger touch whenever you need great speed and dexterity. Trouble arises when speed, dexterity, and loudness are all required. It is for this reason that hard practice of scales, arpeggios, and exercises is necessary. You need as much strength in your fingers as you can muster, but that strength must be directed towards making the key move as quickly as possible through the set-off point, not towards hitting, and remaining on, the key bed.

Strength is certainly required, but there is also a skill in converting that strength into speed at just the right moment to make a loud sound. Finger drumming on some flat surface such as a table is a useful exercise in rehearsing this skill. You will need to be sitting in a playing position, and the surface on which you are practising should, most times at least, be hard. Drum your fingers on the hard surface and try to make as much sound as you can. Do not use your arm to assist your fingers in any way, other than to keep them in the playing position. Use your fingers and your thumbs in this exercise and try to make all your fingers strike with the same strength and speed.

You will almost certainly notice that your fourth and fifth fingers are weaker than the others. It does no harm to exercise these more frequently and more strongly than the others. Do not stop when your fingers begin to feel tired. Always go on just a bit longer. Stopping when they feel tired will not extend them beyond their normal capacity, and it is this extension of normal capacity that you are seeking, but be careful not to strain your fingers too much.

You can also practise finger drumming on your own knee. This has the advantages that you can practise whenever you like (provided those around you do not think you have gone peculiar) and that you can judge the strength of each blow quite accurately by the impact it makes on your knee. I have done more useful finger practice during boring meetings, less than enlivening lessons, and tedious sermons than I care to admit. All you need is sufficient cover so that no one can see your fingers, but beware – you can become so engrossed in your practice that you miss large chunks of the meeting, lesson, or sermon; only you can decide how good or bad that is!

Although it is usual to employ whole arm touch for loud playing and finger touch for light and delicate passages, there are other ways of thinking about touch than just that large and strong means loud. The stronger and more powerful the muscles being used, the greater the control it is possible to exercise over them. Forearm, and whole arm, touch can be appropriate for very quiet passages, and very good effects are obtainable provided the playing speed is slow enough to make it possible. Increased control over the key speed enables us not only to play very softly, but also to make many subtle changes in the dynamics with the minimum of effort. It is up to each of us to decide what form of touch we think is suitable for a particular passage, and, when in doubt, it is best to experiment with a few types before deciding. Our own self-organising system can also be brought into play. A clear aural pre-perception of the sound we wish to produce can help our muscles to make right decisions on how to attain that sound, provided we know something about touch, and about the mechanical efficiency of the particular instrument. But beware: self-organising systems need to be carefully monitored. Because it is their function to relieve us of decision making, they can take over to such an extent that we have played something before we have really controlled it in the way we want. The result of this can be playing which is mechanical and lacking the fine gradations of sound which are the hallmarks of an accomplished pianist.

It is important to remember that, when playing softly, key speed will be slower than when playing loudly. This being so, the actual amount of time needed to play the notes is fractionally *longer*. If you check the speed of your quiet playing by using a metronome, you will find yourself under pressure to keep to the beat. When playing loudly we tend to get faster because key speed needs to be faster. In checking your loud playing against a metronome, the pressure will be on to stop gaining speed. These are not the only reasons for gaining or losing speed; interpretative factors also play a part and you may need carefully to distinguish between such reasons.

Questions

1   *What effect can key dip have on tone production?*
2   *Explain the ambiguity which often arises over the use of the word 'tone'?*
3   *Over which factors in the production of piano sound and tone do we have control?*
4   *On what does the loudness of piano sound depend?*

5   *How can careful listening eventually help us to control our actions?*

6   (a) *Explain what is meant by a balanced arm.*

        (b) *How can we acquire the correct feeling for a balanced arm?*

7   (a) *What do the terms finger touch, hand or wrist touch, forearm touch, and whole arm touch mean?*

        (b) *Describe the movements for each of these touches.*

8   (a) *Which of these touches might you often use in its pure form?*

        (b) *Why are touches more likely to be used in combination rather than pure?*

9   *What is meant by controlled collapse, and why is it helpful?*

10   *Describe weight transfer touch.*

11   *Why is it desirable in practising weight transfer touch to keep the volume high at first?*

12   (a) *How might you practise to simulate the continuity of weight transfer touch when playing melodies which contain wide leaps?*

        (b) *What are the dangers to guard against in trying to do this?*

13   (a) *What is staccato?*

        (b) *How should you approach, and how should you quit a staccato note?*

        (c) *What is the difference between staccato and staccatissimo?*

14   *Describe the various ways of playing staccato.*

15   *What is meant by non legato?*

16   *How does non legato differ from staccato?*

17   (a) *What is meant by forearm rotation?*

        (b) *Describe the preliminary exercises for acquiring a reliable technique for forearm rotation.*

        (c) *List some of the uses of forearm rotation.*

18 (a) What is vibrato technique?
    (b) For what is vibrato technique particularly effective?
19 What is one of the best ways to avoid stiffness?
20 Why is keeping your arm in a balanced state so important?
21 What is the importance of keeping your fingers in line with the keys?
22 How can forward and backward movements over the keys help you to play the right notes?
23 When leaping to a low or high note, what are the important points to remember?
24 Why can it be advantageous, when using hand or wrist touch, to let your hand droop slightly below wrist level?
25 What difficulties can arise when both dexterity and loudness are required when using finger touch?
26 How can you help to strengthen your fingers?
27 (a) What other skill is also required when converting finger strength into speed?
    (b) How can you rehearse this skill?
28 What other ways of thinking about touch are there that don't assume only that more muscle equates to greater loudness?
29 Why is it important to remember that the key speed will be slower when playing softly than when playing loudly?

Chapter 6:

Tone Production

From the previous chapter it is clear that the word tone as applied to piano playing can be ambiguous. Since the actual tone quality of the instrument is established at the time of manufacture, the purpose of the present chapter is to discuss ways of making the best of that tone using the types of touch already described.

Quality of tone is something which almost everyone recognises, especially when it is poor. But what makes tone good or bad? A weed has been described as a plant growing in the wrong place. Although there might be nothing wrong with the plant itself, it is in the wrong place. Much the same might, under certain circumstances, be said of pianistic tone quality. It is its appropriateness to its surroundings which makes it good or bad. Dictionary definitions of tone such as "a musical or vocal sound considered with reference to its quality, as acute or grave, sweet or harsh, loud or soft, clear or dull" do not help us as practising musicians. In trying to capture in words the essence of something which, although recognisable, can have no real verbal equivalent, we are bound to hit trouble.

The sound of a trumpet is distinctive, but it would be impossible to give an adequate verbal description of it to someone who had never before heard it. By using a variety of adjectives, certain comparisons between its sound and that of other instruments could be attempted, but the result would not be wholly satisfactory. Similarly, with pianistic tone, we would be unable to find words to do justice to it in all its diversity. My job in committing advice about the production of 'good' or 'appropriate' tone quality to paper is, therefore, not easy. Demonstration is by far the best way of helping, so being at a disadvantage in that respect I will eventually be calling upon you to do your own demonstrations. Since adjectives are not precise enough for our purposes, I will need to get down to whatever facts are available about tone itself.

Action of the Hammer – Brief Resumé

Before proceeding further, a brief resumé, couched in simple terms, of what actually happens when a piano hammer strikes a string, will help in the understanding of how tone quality is achieved. In common with many instruments, the piano's vibrating system is coupled. Its elements are a string set in motion by a hammer and a soundboard, the two being coupled by a bridge which is firmly attached to the soundboard and over which the string passes. Before it is struck, the string is at rest. When the hammer strikes, shock waves travel in both directions along the string and are transmitted via the bridge to the soundboard, along which they will travel in all directions. Since the hammer strikes at about $\frac{1}{7}$ to $\frac{1}{9}$ of the distance from the nut (tuning pin end), the shock waves will travel different distances to each of the fixed ends of the string before being reflected back along its length, meeting and conflicting with each other before finally settling into a dying pattern of vibration. At the same time, the soundboard will be reacting similarly, but in its own time, to the vibrations from the string, until it too settles into a dying pattern of vibration.

My resumé, as well as being brief, is also a simplification. I have described what would happen to one string; on a piano this is complicated by the fact that it is only the lowest notes which are produced by a single string, the others are produced from two, or three strings tuned in unison. Add to this the brightness which is inherent in steel strings and the result is tone which, at least initially, is made up of many different sounds in conflict with each other. This initial conflict of sound, which can easily be heard when you strike a key, is called the 'starting transient'. It is quite violent but short-lived and following it the sound does not stay steady, immediately dying away until it disappears entirely.

There has also been considerable debate about whether or not pianists can control the quality, or tone, of the sound they produce. I made reference to this problem when discussing 'touch' in the previous chapter by stating that no matter how pianists depress the piano keys, the 'tone' quality of the instrument cannot be altered. Musicians have always maintained that control of tone quality is possible. Scientists, however, have been sceptical of this, although they themselves have gone some way to reconciling the two views by pointing out that the speed at which the hammer strikes the string governs the effect of the starting transient so that there can be some control of the harshness caused.

Elements of Tone Production

The speed of the hammer controls the loudness of the sound and its harshness, but there is one further element which has a considerable effect on the wider aspects of tone control, and that is note length.

There are many excellent books available which describe the elements of piano technique and tone production, but it is not always made clear that all we as pianists can do, once the correct note has been found, is to make that note either louder or softer, longer or shorter. All pianistic effects (apart from some special ones which can be gained by the use of pedals) are controlled by variations in dynamics and note lengths. This is not a suggestion that the well-considered advice contained in books on general muscular control, on playing scales, arpeggios and octaves, or producing legato and staccato effects, vibration technique, and the many other technical aspects which they cover, should be ignored, but rather it is a plea that when the advice has been read and understood, the pianist's attention should be focused on the control of the two variables: volume and length.

Looking more closely at the fundamentals involved, note lengths can be fairly readily controlled, but the fine grading of dynamics is more difficult. Loudness depends on the speed at which a key is depressed; the faster the key speed the louder the sound, but also the greater the harshness.

Control of Loud and Soft Sounds

Soft sounds, which depend on a slow key speed, are more difficult to control than louder ones. The reason for this is that students tend to hold back when trying to play softly. They are almost afraid to touch the keys, with the result that some notes do not sound at all, and many of those that do are of indifferent tone

quality. Holding back is fatal to good, clear tone production. The reason is the purely physical one of the
piano's construction. The 'dip' of a piano key, that is,
the distance it travels from a position of rest to one
where it is fully depressed and touching the keybed, is
about 1cm or ⅜". A pianist, therefore, has a very short
distance in which to control tone production.

But this is only part of the story. About half way
through the key's travel there is the set-off point at
which the hammer is flicked upwards (in a grand
piano) or forward (in an upright piano) to strike the
string. When the key has passed this set off point the
pianist can have no further control over that particular
strike. It is therefore imperative that the key is travelling at exactly the right speed, at about the half way
point of the key dip, to produce the desired loudness.
If it is not travelling fast enough to set off the striking
action correctly, the result will be either a very insipid
sound or even no sound at all. If, however, the key is
travelling too fast, the sound produced will be too
loud. The only way to produce a soft sound of good
quality is to experiment with key speeds, remembering
that it is the speed at which the key goes through the
set-off point which is important.

Having, by experiment, 'felt' the exact muscular sen-
sation needed to induce the key speed for the sound
you want, and practised it carefully many times, you
must be able to reproduce it whenever that particular
quality of sound is needed. Since you only have something like ³⁄₁₆" to ¼" or 5 to 7.5mm of travel to
accomplish what you want, you must decide on the key
speed either at (risky), or just above, key level and then
make a positive movement right through the set-off
point and down to the key bed. You have no time for a

change of mind. Any holding back when the distances involved are so small must result in at best faulty, or at worst non-existent, tone.

To attain the appropriate key speed, fine gradations of muscular control are needed. There are many books on the subject, but the important thing to remember about touch is that the deed is done in that short distance just described, so the muscular conditions must be exactly right a split second before that key begins to descend. If they are not, the tone you produce will be poor.

Demonstration of Piano Tone

Loudness and Softness

Since the control of loudness, softness, and note length are the only facilities at the disposal of the pianist, good tone, whatever that might be, must result from the carefully balanced mixture of these factors. This is where I must now call on you to act as demonstrator. Strike the B flat almost an octave above middle C as strongly as you can and, whilst holding the note down, listen carefully to the dying sound. Depending on the resonance of the instrument you have, it will take about 15 to 20 seconds for the note to die away completely. During that time you can hear the full range of the piano's tone 'colour'. The initial sound will be 'rough' or 'harsh' (the starting transient) because of the sudden displacement of the string and the resultant conflict of the vibrations. The inharmonious elements will soon disappear leaving as full and rich a tone as the instrument can give. The tone will gradually soften into a gentle hum and finally into a faint whisper before dissolving into silence, the exact moment at which it stops being difficult to establish. Try the experiment a few times, listening very carefully to the changes in 'quality' as the volume of sound dies. After listening a few times to the B flat above middle C, try the B flat immediately below middle C and become aware of its various tone qualities. Try the same experiment with each B flat on the keyboard. The differences in the lengths of time it takes for each note to die will be considerable, and the higher the pitch the more difficult it becomes to make a full, rich, sonorous, and durable tone. Having listened to the tone qualities which your piano can produce, practise striking various notes at different pitches and see if you make them give you exactly the sound you are aiming for.

The value of the exercise comes from listening intently, and in teaching yourself how to form an aural picture of the sound a note will produce before you actually strike it. Just as it was important to give yourself sufficient thinking time to get the right finger to the right note, so too is sufficient thinking time needed during practice in tone production to ensure that each note is struck at the correct speed to produce a suitable tone for its position in the music. Practise producing various degrees of loudness using pure finger, pure hand, pure forearm, and pure whole arm touches as described in the previous chapter, as well as combinations of touches, and try to imagine just before you strike the note exactly what the tone quality will be.

Note Length

Having practised for loudness, the next exercise is to listen to the effect of length on notes of different degrees of loudness. A succession of notes played loudly and of short duration will sound crisp and clear by comparison with notes of a similar loudness held for a longer time. The latter will sound loud, or ponderous, or majestic, depending on the adjective you choose to use. The actual loudness appears to be less when the notes are shorter in length, but the brightness and crispness is greater. Soft notes of short duration will appear to sound even quieter than those of a similar intensity held longer. Time spent listening to the effects of loudness and length on single notes will pay dividends in your playing. Building up a repertory of sounds which you can clearly imagine before they are heard will help you to aim exactly for the required sound, allowing you to make subtle alterations to what we call tone. Gone will be the days of just loud and soft, or take it as it comes.

So far discussion has been focused on single notes, but piano music usually consists of chords, and melodies which are interwoven, resulting in notes sounding together. Under these circumstances it is the 'definition' of the chord, or the supremacy of a particular note or musical line which 'defines' the tone quality. It is seldom the case that every note in a chord is given the same intensity. One or two notes usually take precedence, adding life and interest to the texture and thereby enhancing the quality of the playing, and the quality of the tone.

There are many reasons for making one or more notes louder than others. It is open to debate as to whether such features should be discussed in connection with tone production or under the general heading of interpretation, but they do alter what we call the tonal quality and so need to be discussed here. The carefully thought out balance of loudness between notes which are sounding simultaneously is therefore an important element in tone production. This balance is achieved by knowing which notes to subdue as much as which notes to highlight.

It is possible to bring a note into prominence by volume, or length, or both. Making the prominent note louder is usually the first thought that comes to mind, but increases in volume can lead to harshness rather than importance, unless they are carefully controlled. Although we are again bordering on the realm of interpretation, my real objective here is to suggest how tone can be altered by highlighting, rather than the use and intensity of such highlighting in any particular piece of music; it is the method used that needs to be explored.

Training yourself to make one note in a chord more prominent than the others, although not difficult, demands careful and detailed practice. The easiest notes in a chord to highlight are either the highest or the lowest. The inner notes can be more awkward, but perseverance once the principles have been established, will produce the desired result.

Highlighting the Top Note of a Chord

Let us assume, for demonstration purposes, that the chord you are about to play contains the three notes E, G, and C immediately above middle C (technically, a chord must consist of three or more different notes). You are going to play these notes with your right hand, finger 1 (thumb) on E, finger 2 (index finger) on G, and finger 5 (little finger) on C, and it is the note C played with finger 5 that you wish to make more prominent than the others.

Place your fingers over the three notes in question as if you are ready to play them all. Lift your hand, and in the balanced state, extend finger 5 down towards the key. Still keeping in the playing position for all three notes, rotate your hand very slightly towards finger 5 and then bring it down, using forearm touch, onto the keys so that you play *only* the note C, the other two fingers being above the notes E and G, but too high above them to touch. Let your arm weight rest on note C while holding the note down, and "feel" the amount of weight you are applying to it. Lift your hand, then bring it down again to play only the note C. Make sure that your hand descends at a steady speed, that finger 5 goes right down to the bottom of the key, and that it stays firm (i.e. does not collapse) when the key comes into contact with the key bed. The sound you produce must be firm and loud (there should be neither weakness nor harshness) and you should again feel the amount of weight on your little finger. As explained in the previous chapter, do not press on the key; instead, by releasing tension in your upper arm and shoulder, allow the weight of your hand and arm to rest on it and let your little finger support that weight. There should, of course, be no feeling of weight on your other two fingers because they are not in contact with their respective keys. Do this a few times, directing all your weight on, and attention to, your little finger. That little finger should feel as if it is supporting a heavy weight.

This might seem a ludicrously simple exercise, hardly worth practising. Don't you believe it. I did point out a few paragraphs earlier that this work needed *careful* and *detailed* practice, so do not skimp on the details. The important points to establish about the exercise so far are:

(a) Your hand must work as one whole unit, and your fingers must stay in the relative positions you intend.

(b) When your hand, propelled by your forearm, comes down onto the keys, your little finger must go right down to the key bed without checking at any point once you have started the movement.

(c) Your hand must be brought down at a constant speed, capable of producing a sound at least *f* in volume.

(d) You must feel the weight of your hand and arm being supported by a little finger which does not give way under the strain.

We now move on to a more difficult step. You are going to aim almost to play your thumb and first finger while continuing to play strongly with your little finger. By almost, I mean that your thumb and first finger will actually come into contact with their respective keys but will not make them sound. This requires considerable accuracy in aiming. Using forearm touch, practise bringing your hand down onto the keys in such a way that your little finger still plays its C firmly, but that your other two fingers stop at key surface level and go no further. Your hand must be brought down without its speed being checked at any point. Once you have started the action, your hand, as before, must be kept moving constantly until your little finger hits the key bed. When it does so, check the other two fingers to see that they are at key surface level. Resist the temptation to cheat – what you are rehearsing here is a very accurate movement, so deceiving yourself will not help. This stage is important because when you actually play the full chord the notes should not, perceptibly, be split – all the notes must appear to sound simultaneously, which means that your aim and your judgment of finger positions must be exactly right. In practice, the prominent note will usually strike fractionally before the others, but it should never noticeably do so.

When you have rehearsed this action a few times, try the next, difficult, step of making the E and G played by thumb and second finger sound very softly whilst your little finger still plays the C strongly. To do this, play once more with your thumb and second finger just contacting the keys and little finger playing the C firmly. Leave your hand on the keys in that position, then lower your thumb and second finger just enough to depress their respective keys beyond the set-off point, and almost as far as the key bed. Keeping your hand in that position, use your forearm to lift it and to play all three notes, making sure that you concentrate your main effort on your little finger which should feel to be supporting the weight of your hand, while your other two fingers should feel as though they are not carrying any real weight. Practise this many times concentrating your effort on:

(a) Making the note C played by your little finger sing out strongly and clearly.
(b) Making the other two notes sound, but only very softly.
(c) Making all three notes, either sound, or appear to sound, together, with no obvious splitting.

It takes many words to describe what to do, even though the actions themselves are simple. But what is not simple is acquiring the fine judgment necessary to get the end result right. If the E and G are sounding too loudly, practise the second stage exercise a few more times, and at the conclusion of each rehearsal of it extend your thumb and first finger to a position just beyond the set-off point and just above the key bed. Do this over and over again until you feel sure you have estimated accurately the height your thumb and first finger should be. Remember, you do not want them to hit the key bed with the same force as does your little finger, but at the same time they must go past the set-off point for making their notes speak. The judgment is critical.

You will probably find that you get it right sometimes and not others. Try to remember how your hand and fingers "feel" when you get it right. When you get it wrong, analyse what went wrong with it. Did you rotate your hand slightly towards your thumb? Was your second finger extended too far so that it came down too soon, or was it not extended sufficiently and so did not produce a note at all? Was your little finger extended so much that it came down before the others, thus splitting the chord? Self analysis, when you are playing only three notes, will not present much of a problem. Get used to doing it so that you are well equipped to tackle chords with a greater number of notes.

Highlighting the Bottom Note of a Chord

When you can highlight with your little finger, transfer your attention to your thumb. Using the processes described above, practise making the thumb note more prominent than the others. Being stronger than your little finger, your thumb might respond more quickly to the task, but it might also split the chord more frequently.

Highlighting the Middle Note of a Chord

Highlighting your 2nd (index) finger on note G is likely to be the most difficult of all, since the two fingers you are wishing to subdue are not alongside each other. You cannot on this occasion rotate towards the note you are wishing to highlight since it is in the middle. Make sure that finger 2 is extended and you can feel the weight on it; there should be no weight on fingers 1 and 5. If you are having trouble, extend finger 2 so that it strikes before the others, splitting the chord, and feel the weight at knuckle level. Withdraw your 2nd finger a little for the next strike and aim at reducing the weight you feel at knuckle level. Keep on reducing this weight until the chord comes together sufficiently to make the splitting disappear, while still allowing the note G to remain highlighted. Keep trying, it can be done.

Do not wait until you have mastered the technique with your right hand before practising it with your left. To use the same fingering pattern, that is fingers 1, 2, and 5, practise with thumb on middle C, finger 2 on the A below, and finger 5 on the E below that. The procedures for learning are, of course, just the same as they were for your right hand.

When you become used to highlighting in this way, try playing chords in each hand using different, and more difficult, patterns of fingering. Decide which note you wish to highlight and see how often you are successful. Notes played with the 4th finger are usually the most difficult to highlight.

Once you have mastered the technique using single chords in each hand, a useful exercise is to take a four part setting of a hymn or carol and then highlight each of the vocal lines, soprano, alto, tenor, and bass, in turn.

To produce a musical effect make the voice you are highlighting as legato and song-like as possible. To achieve this, the accompanying voices should be played in a delicate non legato style. This allows your highlighted legato melody to 'shine through' all the time, and its continuity will enhance its prominence over the rest. Do not allow the 'gaps' in your non legato playing to be too clearly heard. They should be so discreet that a listener cannot detect how it is that the melody appears to be sounding out so smoothly and yet the chords are changing. What you are really doing is allowing your melody notes almost to overlap each other. This demands very careful judgment on your part and you need to be aware that your highlighted melody is singing out on its own for a split second while the other parts are silent. Judicious use of the sustaining pedal can also assist, but blurring must be avoided. With practice and very careful listening, you will be able to give a reasonable performance giving prominence to any part you choose. The secret always is to subdue the parts which are not being highlighted; the non legato style of playing them helps this, and avoids the temptation to play the prominent part *ff*.

Highlighting in Other Circumstances

I have spent some time describing how to highlight one note in a chord, but the technique you will have learned is also useful for making melodies, or motives, prominent in circumstances which do not involve chords. If the melody of the piece you are learning is in the uppermost part make sure that it is gently highlighted to sound slightly louder than the other parts, and that it is fingered in such a way that it can be played more legato than the others too. It is not usually necessary to make it very much louder, but a listener's ear needs to focus on something; the slight increase in volume of the melody, coupled with the legato playing, will produce the desired effect. It is our job as pianists to make sure that we bring the most important elements of the music to the listener's notice by subtlety and artistry, rather than brute force. Exactly what these elements are will vary throughout the piece because, even if the melody is in the uppermost part, there will be points of interest elsewhere in the texture of the music. They may consist, among other things, of counter melodies, colourful harmonies, arresting rhythmic patterns, or interesting bass lines. These should be gently highlighted, not to the exclusion of the predominant melody, but rather as an enhancement to it.

These little fluctuations of dynamics and note length, which cause any particular feature of the music to be made prominent, all add up to what we mean by "tone". If, suddenly, a few notes gently sing out above the others, only to die away again to make way for some other point of interest, the music is given life, definition, and an extra dimension, lifting it above the ordinary. It must not be forgotten, however, that music often needs periods when nothing appears to be happening in preparation for some point of climax, or feature of interest, to come.

Questions

1   *How does a knowledge of what happens when a hammer strikes a piano string help in understanding tone quality?*
2   *(a) What is meant by the scientific term 'starting transient'?*

(b)   *How does the starting transient affect tone?*

3   *What three elements have a considerable effect on what we call tone?*

4   *Which two variables govern the sound we can produce from a note?*

5   *Why is holding back fatal to good, clear tone production?*

6   (a)   *What is meant by the term 'key dip'?*

    (b)   *Why is it important that the 'key dip' is neither too deep nor too shallow?*

7   *What do you understand by the term 'set-off point'?*

8   *Why is it important that the key is travelling at just the right speed when it passes through the set-off point?*

9   *Once you have decided what key speed you need, why do you not have time for a change of mind?*

10   *What can you gain from listening intently to the dying sound of a note you have struck strongly?*

11   *Why should you try the experiment with notes of different pitch?*

12   *What is the advantage of trying to form an aural picture of the sound of a note before you strike it?*

13   *What will you gain from practice in producing various degrees of loudness using pure finger, pure hand, pure forearm, and pure whole arm touches?*

14   *What difference might note length make to sound quality?*

15   *How can interest be achieved when notes are grouped into chords, or into interwoven melodies?*

16   *How can the highlighting of a note, or notes, be achieved?*

17   (a)   *Outline a programme for training yourself to high-light the top note of a chord.*

    (b)   *How can you adapt the same training programme to highlight middle and bottom notes of a chord?*

18   *In what circumstances, other than chord playing, might highlighting be used to advantage?*

Chapter 7:

Phrasing

Before commenting on phrasing, it is necessary to say something about the form and structure of music. If you have not had any formal training in the theory of music, parts of the following information might at first be difficult for you. There are other books available which deal specifically with musical forms and my brief explanations will help you to understand the rest.

All musical structures are built up from certain basic elements: notes, bars, phrases, and sentences. These are combined, contrasted and moulded into entities of greater length, and eventually turned into individual pieces or movements of even larger works. Some of these individual pieces or movements are in the shape of 'set piece' musical forms such as binary (two-section form), ternary (three-section form), rondo (a musical form in which a particular melody keeps returning), and sonata form (a much more complex musical structure having elements of both binary and ternary shapes), whilst others are made up of looser combinations of the basic elements.

Accentuation and Punctuation

Whatever the structure of the piece we are playing, we must make sense of the elements from which it is built. Music, like poetry, depends on accentuation, usually indicated by punctuation, to convey its meaning. These two terms need some explanation from a musical point of view if their full importance is to be understood. Taking accentuation first, this has already been mentioned in Chapter 6, Tone Production, where the two factors of loudness and length were discussed. It was pointed out that an increase in volume is not the only way to achieve prominence – note length can also be an important factor. A long note in a melody, regardless of its volume, assumes greater importance than a short note of similar volume, and this greater importance can be felt as an accent. A note following a short period of silence can appear to be accentuated, as can one which follows a phrase ending which has diminished in volume. Almost anything which brings a note or chord specifically to the attention of the listener can act like an accent. Defining clearly any unexpected harmonies, or suddenly decreasing volume, particularly if the note concerned comes fractionally after its anticipated beat, are just some of the many ways in which a note can be brought into prominence; regular progress from accent to accent, however that accent is created, gives shape to the music.

Musical Punctuation – Cadences

Every language needs punctuation to make it intelligible, and the language of music is no exception. Musical punctuation is accomplished by cadences, or phrase endings, which are recognisable patterns, or progressions, of pairs of chords. There are four main cadences: perfect, plagal, imperfect, and interrupted. Perfect and plagal cadences can be used at the end of any musical phrase or sentence, and as the concluding chords of any work or part of a work. Imperfect and interrupted cadences, because they lack the finality of the other two, are used where a less definite ending is required, in much the same way as, in writing, a comma might be used rather than a full stop. The most obvious use of cadences can be seen and heard in hymn tunes, because a cadence of some sort appears at the end of each line. The final line will most likely, but not invariably, end with a perfect, or a plagal, cadence, whereas the other lines can end with any cadence. Hymn tunes and short pieces often remain firmly rooted in one key only, in which case the perfect and plagal cadences come to rest on that key chord. Imperfect and interrupted cadences come to rest on chords other than the key chord, contributing to their lack of finality. If you happen to play the hymn *O God Our Help in Ages Past* you will notice an unusual cadence at the end of the third line. This is a Phrygian cadence and it also appears quite often at the end of baroque period slow movements in minor keys which are followed by a movement in a major key, although it is not generally included in most descriptions of cadences. (The term baroque is used to denote music written from about 1600 to 1750.)

A perfect cadence.

A phrase, ending with the same perfect cadence.

Various Uses of the Word 'Phrase'

Turning now more directly to the main substance of this chapter, the word "phrase" can appear in different contexts when discussing musical matters. It is therefore necessary to show the similarities and the differences in its use so that confusion can be avoided. The three main ways in which it is used are:

(a) As an element in musical construction and analysis;
(b) As a marking on musical scores;
(c) As an interpretative factor in performance.

In all instances, a phrase consists of notes grouped in such a way that they have some definite connection with each other. Since the reasons for that connection are not necessarily the same in all three cases, each one will be dealt with separately.

An Element in Musical Construction

Starting with its use in musical construction and analysis first, a phrase is a group of approximately four bars which makes a musical unit ending in a cadence. I used the word approximately, because four bar phrases are the most common, but irregular phrases containing more, or fewer, bars are also possible. Musical phrases work in a similar way to phrases in poetry. They encapsulate certain elements of the argument and, although they are not complete in themselves, when coupled with other phrases, can form longer and more complete entities in the form of sentences. Many phrases can be broken down into smaller units called motifs, or figures. These are often characteristic elements in the context of the music; the rhythmic and melodic figure based on the morse code call sign for the letter V (. . . –) used at the opening of the first movement of Beethoven's fifth symphony is a case in point.

The rhythmic and melodic figure from Beethoven's fifth symphony.

The skill needed to be able to analyse music, and to work out its phrase, sentence, and motivic structure, is one which all aspiring pianists should acquire. Without it, it is not possible, unaided, to come to a true understanding of the music. Taking an example from literature, it is only when properly punctuated that on paper the following verse from a well–known poem is truly intelligible:

Break, break, break on.
Thy cold grey stones O sea and I would.
That my tongue could utter.
The thoughts that arise within me.

Reciting this extract from Tennyson in a monotone, without emphases, and, as I have written it out above, stopping at every full stop as if it were the end of something, it does not make sense. Since we know the meaning of the words, we can alter their groupings so that the above lines make sense. However, someone who could do no more than make the sounds for the words and had no idea of their meaning, could not. Without a knowledge of musical structure, or without relying on the expertise of someone who has that knowledge, we could, in our playing, commit howlers similar to those I have made in my faulty punctuation of the lines from Tennyson and, what is worse, we might not be aware that we are doing so.

Phrase Markings on a Score

The second use of the word phrase concerns the marks of phrasing that appear on copies of piano, and other, music. Much depends on the philosophy of the editor (or the composer) as to how these markings are used in any particular piece of music. In most instances, the phrase marks which cover four bars (occasionally two if the bars in question are long) serve a structural purpose, indicating the main points of punctuation. The marks showing shorter phrases are often referred to as slurs. The markings for both long phrases and for slurs are interpretative aids, indicating accentuations which might run counter to those suggested by the bar lines.

Phrasing as a Factor in Performance

The third, and most usual, meaning of phrase concerns its use as an interpretative factor in performance.

When we refer to someone phrasing well or badly, this is the sense in which we are using the word. But since the phrases are already established by the composer and marked by the editor, what is it, precisely, that we mean by phrasing?

Making, Shaping, Building, or Turning a Phrase

Since it is the performer's duty to bring to life the written musical symbols and markings, every phrase, no matter how clearly established or marked on paper, must be re-made at each performance. Because of this it might be more accurate to refer to making a phrase, shaping a phrase, building a phrase, or turning a phrase, rather than obscure the issue by blanket use of the word phrasing.

General Guidance on Treating Phrases in Performance

Our task is to bring out the shape of each phrase by our mode of performance. The most usual advice given is to build the phrase up to a point of climax, probably somewhere about two thirds to three quarters of the way through it, and then allow it to fall to a point of repose at its end, or cadence. Since each phrase is an individual entity, this order of shaping does not hold good for every one, but it embodies some basic principles common to all. A phrase must have a clear beginning and ending and it must be perceptibly separated from the phrases surrounding it. Within the phrase itself there must be points of climax and points of repose. Where these points occur differs from phrase to phrase, but they must be present, and it is the build up towards the climaxes and the subsequent relaxation when moving away from them that gives life to the music.

Questions

1   From what basic elements are all musical structures built?

2   In what ways, other than by increasing volume, can a note be accentuated?

3   How is musical punctuation accomplished?

4   In what type of musical composition are cadences most obvious?

5   What is a 'phrase'?

6   What are the various musical uses of the word 'phrase'?

7   (a) Why is it highly desirable for pianists to analyse the music they are playing?

    (b) What is the danger of not being able to do so?

8   What is the purpose of phrase marks on a musical score?

9   What is meant by the term 'phrasing' as a factor in performance?

10   Why might it be better to refer to making, shaping, building, or turning a phrase rather than just using the term 'phrasing'?

11   Why is it important to find the beginnings and ends of phrases in the music we are playing?

12   Having found its beginning and its end, how might we set about giving the phrase shape?

13   (a) Where, approximately, is the most usual climactic point in a phrase?

    (b) Do all phrases conform to this pattern?

Chapter 8:

Pedalling

It has already been stated in Chapter 1 that there are usually two, sometimes three, pedals on a piano. The descriptions given there were offered as assistance when buying a piano, but some more detailed explanation of what they actually do would seem appropriate before discussing their use. It will be better to start with instruments with only two pedals, since they are most common. The left pedal is referred to as the soft pedal, and the right, as the loud pedal. Although the terms 'soft' and 'loud' have some relevance, they are not entirely helpful. A much greater understanding of what the pedals actually do is needed if we are to use them to their best advantage.

The Soft Pedal

There are three distinct and different types of soft pedal available. By far the most effective is the *una corda* type. Depending on their pitch, piano notes are produced by one, two, or three strings. The notes in the lowest, or bass, register have one heavily weighted string; those in the middle, or tenor, register have two strings; and those in the high, or treble, register, have three strings. The *una corda* mechanism, which moves the whole keyboard slightly to the right when the pedal is depressed, has two effects. In the tenor register, it allows the hammers to hit only one of the two strings; and in the treble register, two of the three strings. But in all three registers, it allows the softer, less used, areas of the hammer face to strike the strings. This results in a totally different quality of sound, certainly softer, but also of a different timbre (tone quality) from that produced when the pedal is not depressed.

The *una corda* type of mechanism is used on grand pianos, and occasionally on uprights, but the most usual type of soft pedal mechanism on uprights instead moves the hammers forward, closer to the string. This restricts the distance, and therefore the speed of the hammer's 'throw', so reducing the volume of sound. Unfortunately it does not alter its timbre.

The third type of soft pedal mechanism is more primitive than either of the others. It introduces a strip of felt between the hammers and the strings, reducing the volume of sound, but robbing it of much of its quality.

A similar device is sometimes available on modern instruments and worked by a third pedal placed between the normal two. It introduces a thick strip of felt between the hammers and the strings, greatly reducing both volume and sound quality. It is usually called a practice pedal.

The Loud, Sustaining, or Damper Pedal

The so-called loud pedal is better described as the sustaining, or damper, pedal, because it raises all the dampers, allowing the strings to vibrate freely. If you were to depress this pedal and, keeping it depressed, play any short piece, you would soon realise the importance of the dampers. Without them all the notes, chords, and harmonies come together, producing one chaotic blur of sound; the eminent piano teacher Tobias Matthay's reason for saying that "the pedal is to stop the sound".

The Sostenuto Pedal

There is one other type of mechanism which affects the dampers, and that is the sostenuto pedal. Like the practice pedal, it is placed between the two usual pedals. Its purpose is to hold up only those dampers which are raised at the time the pedal is depressed, leaving the other dampers in contact with the strings. The raised dampers will remain raised until the sostenuto pedal is released. While the sostenuto pedal is in operation, the sustaining pedal can be used in the normal way. This facility allows a note or chord to be sustained without interfering with any other notes or chords which might be played, released, or pedalled, while it is being operated.

The two outer pedals on a piano are always the same: left for *una corda* (or its equivalent) and right for sustaining. If a middle pedal is fitted, it might be either the practice type, or the sostenuto type, although I have on one occasion played a piano on which the middle pedal brought strips of metal into contact with the strings, supposedly making the instrument sound like a harpsichord.

Use of Pedals

So much for the types of pedal mechanism, for playing purposes it is how these pedals are used that is important.

Una Corda Pedal

When the left pedal is required, the instruction *una corda* appears in the score, and when it is to be released the instruction *tre corde* is given. It does not matter what sort of mechanism your piano's left pedal operates, when you see the instruction *una corda*, use the left pedal, and when you see the instruction *tre corde*, release it. Do not be tempted to use the left pedal when you see the signs *p* or *pp*. Your finger technique should be sufficient to make those dynamic alterations without resorting to mechanical devices. The left (or soft) pedal should be used for special effects, not as a support for inadequate technique. If it is over-used, it will inhibit the development of your technique; and if your piano has a true *una corda* mechanism, over-use of the softer areas of the hammers' face will eventually spoil the *una corda* effect.

Sostenuto Pedal

The sostenuto pedal (see opposite), if your piano has one (and not many instruments do), is useful particularly for playing music by impressionist composers. Debussy, for instance, often asks that a chord be sustained, while at the same time requiring the use of both hands to play other things, and Rachmaninoff does something similar at the beginning of his well-known *Prelude in C sharp minor*, by requiring a double octave to be held while many different harmonies are played above it. If you do not have a sostenuto pedal, effects of this sort need to be done by half pedalling, a technique described on page 115.

Loud or Sustaining Pedal

By far the most important pedal is the sustaining, or damper, pedal. Anton Rubenstein is said to have called it "the soul of the piano", but to be so it must be accurately and sensitively controlled.

It has two main uses. The first, obviously, is to sustain the sound so that a legato effect can be obtained when fingering alone will not suffice. The second is to enhance the sound quality of the instrument by allowing for sympathetic vibration.

Legato Pedalling

This is a useful pedalling technique which should be learned by all pianists. It is essential whenever maintaining a pianistic legato with hands only is impossible. Playing successions of chords, for example, can seldom be accomplished without lifting your hand off the keys from time to time in order to shape your fingering for the next chord. This results in gaps in the continuity, unless you are extremely skilled in leaping from chord to chord without a break in weight transfer. Legato pedalling technique is needed to bridge such gaps satisfactorily. The loud pedal must be depressed to sustain the sound when your hands are off the keys, and released when your hands are on the keys, to prevent blurring.

Try this very simple exercise which will demonstrate in slow motion how to practise legato pedalling. Play, with both hands, a chord of D major with a highlighted A at the top. Put your foot on the damper pedal and lift your hands from the keys. The chord will continue to sound with the top note, A, being

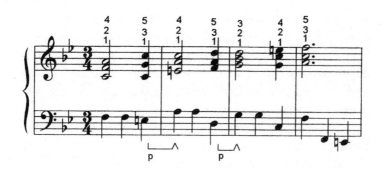

Legato pedalling. Make sure that the pedal is depressed immediately after the notes are struck but while they are still being held down. Release the pedal just as the next chord is played.

prominent. Still keeping the pedal depressed, play a chord of G with a highlighted B at the top and release the pedal just as the chord of G sounds. Depress the pedal again to sustain the G chord and lift your hands from the keys. Now play a chord of C major with a highlighted C at the top, and release the pedal just as the the chord sounds. Depress the pedal again to sustain the C chord and lift your hands from the keys. If you have synchronised your hands and the pedal accurately you should have heard three chords with the short melody formed by the highlighted A, B, and C singing out clearly without a break or overlapping. If your hands and foot were not accurately synchronised there would either be a gap in this short melody, or some of the melody notes would overlap each other.

It is the ability to place a note or chord accurately into the space between releasing and depressing the loud pedal which is the essence of good legato pedalling. During the performance of this short exercise the pedal will have remained depressed for most of the time, having only been released, very briefly, twice. It is helpful to think of legato pedalling in this way. The pedal is depressed for most of the time, only being flicked up and then immediately depressed again to allow the new note or chord to be played.

The considerable degree of synchronisation needed between hand and foot can only be achieved if guided by careful listening. The actions necessary for accurate legato pedalling should be practised frequently. It is not an easy technique to master because hand and foot do not work exactly together. The exercise I have suggested is very short and you will have sufficient time to depress and release the pedal. In the course of a piece of music this time is limited, so during practice it is therefore necessary to get used to making the actions as quick and as accurate as you can. It might take some time to acquire the knack, but keep trying: the final effects will make your efforts worthwhile.

Direct Pedalling

It can be desirable on occasions to depress the sustaining pedal *with* the note or chord you are playing, rather than after it. This is sometimes referred to as direct pedalling. It is useful when playing detached chords, or when the note you are wishing to catch with the pedal needs to be quitted immediately. The beginning of an arpeggio pattern, or when a low note is followed immediately by a chord in a much higher register of the instrument, as is necessary in some accompaniment patterns (particularly in waltzes), are cases in point.

Half Pedalling

The term does not mean that a pedal is to be brought half way up. It refers to the correct use of the sustaining pedal to achieve effects that would otherwise require a sostenuto pedal. The thicker, heavier strings of the low notes require a greater amount of damping than do the lighter treble strings. The loud pedal must be *fully* raised for a fraction of a second and then *fully* depressed again so as to obliterate the higher notes and allow the lower ones to continue sounding. As an example of how half pedalling works, with your left hand strike very firmly an octave G, its top note being an octave and a half below middle C, while directly pedalling it. Take your hand off the keys and, with a quick flick of your ankle, raise and lower the sustaining pedal so swiftly that the octave is slightly, but not completely, damped. Continue raising and lowering the sustaining pedal, again with quick flicks of the ankle, and see how often you can do it before you damp the notes completely. Do this exercise a few times to get the feel of the process.

Now play a chord of G, your left hand filling out the octave you have just played with a B and a D, and your right hand playing a similar G chord starting an octave and a half above middle C. Strike the complete chord using both hands simultaneously while directly pedalling it. Take your hands off the keys and, with a quick flick of your ankle, raise and lower the sustaining pedal so swiftly that the sound of the upper chord is damped, but most of the lower chord's sound sings on. Keep on practising this until you can cut the upper chord quickly and completely while still allowing the lower chord to sing on. As mentioned earlier, sections of Rachmaninoff's famous *Prelude in C sharp minor* and many similar passages in other works will benefit from accurate half pedalling.

Sound Enhancement by Use of the Damper Pedal

By raising all the dampers, the strings of many notes which are not actually struck are allowed to resonate in sympathy with those which are. The effect of this increased resonance ranges from giving the tone a slight amount of 'warming' to making it 'shout'.

To make the piano shout, play a chord containing many notes, as loudly as you can, while directly pedalling it. You will then hear the full impact of the starting transient, enhanced by sympathetic resonance from other strings.

The warming effect of the pedal can best be demonstrated by playing a chord without pedal, and, while holding it down, depressing the sustaining pedal. A very slight crescendo will be immediately noticeable, as well as an increased mellowness and greater sonority of tone. This is caused by many strings being allowed to vibrate in sympathy with those which have been struck. Discreet use of this effect allows well controlled crescendos and diminuendos to be made more easily than with fingers alone. But beware, this type of sound can be so addictive that unenhanced notes appear dull by comparison. To be able to mix the 'drier' sound of unpedalled notes satisfactorily with the 'warmer' pedalled notes requires careful listening so that the volume and the length of each sound is controlled. Both sound qualities have their place – it is essential to be able to combine or contrast them as the music dictates.

Questions

1   Why should you resist the temptation to use the una corda pedal whenever you see the signs p or pp?
2   What is the instruction on a copy of music when the left pedal is to be used?
3   What is the purpose of a sostenuto pedal?
4   What pedalling technique will help you simulate the effect of a sostenuto pedal?
5   What are the other names for the so-called loud pedal, and why are they more appropriate?
6   The sustaining pedal has two main uses, what are they?
7   Explain the technique known as legato pedalling.
8   What is direct pedalling and when might it be useful?
9   (a)   What is meant by half pedalling?
     (b)   How can you train yourself to use the technique of half pedalling?
10 How can you make a piano 'shout'?
11 How can you demonstrate the warming effect of the sustaining pedal?

Chapter 9:

Learning a New Piece

Sooner or later, when talking or writing about piano playing, the word interpretation appears. While vaguely covering all the expressive aspects of performance, the word itself gives no clue as to how these aspects are to be achieved. For that reason, in a practical book such as this, an essay on musical interpretation is inappropriate; what is more to the point is discussing, in some detail, the various factors which contribute to making a presentable performance. There are many excellent exhortations in other books about getting to the heart of the music, and making the spirit of the music come alive, and so on, but the following pages will be directed to showing how, by using the technical skills you possess, you can achieve a satisfying standard of performance.

Learning a new piece of music involves many elements which, when they have been worked out, understood, and painstakingly rehearsed, must all come together simultaneously to produce the final result. The problem in writing about these elements is that, apart from a few obvious ones, such as learning the notes, there is not necessarily any definite chronological order in which they should be dealt with. Some need to be considered before you play a note, some stretch right through the whole learning, and even the performing, period, while others are of the "as and when" variety to be dealt with as, or if, required, and also precisely when required. In an attempt to impose some sort of logical and ordered approach, I will deal with those which need to be addressed early in the learning process first, and the others I will leave to your discretion to select when the time is right to consider or incorporate them.

In common with the previous chapters, the information which follows is presented so that it can be applied to any piece of music. A few specific references might occur, but I have avoided the temptation of explaining how to go about something by examining in detail one particular piece of music. This adds to the difficulty of my task, but it does mean that no piece of advice will be given in reference to music whose details are not known to you.

Preliminaries

A few simple, practical things should be done before you begin:

(a) Choose a new piece of music, preferably one which you have never tried to play before. This is desirable so that you do not inherit any bad habits acquired in your previous contact with the music. If it is not possible or desirable to begin on an entirely new piece, you must be prepared for the frequent use of the corrective procedures described in Chapter 3, which will undoubtedly slow down your progress.

(b) It is advantageous to have a piece of music which is reasonably well known to you on hand before you begin your new one. Breaking down a new piece and practising it slowly and carefully is exacting work. It is a help to relieve the concentration at times by switching to something which is well rehearsed, but not yet up to performance standard. As well as relieving the concentration, remembering some of the difficulties encountered in that piece can act as a timely reminder of what to be looking out for in the early stages of learning your new piece.

(c) Always have a pencil and rubber, and possibly also a notebook, available on the piano. It is essential to make accurate records of decisions while practising. It is very easy to forget a fingering which worked well in practice, and it is also necessary to obliterate all evidence of one which did not. A few words jotted down in a notebook can act as a reminder of something you particularly wish to do during your next practice session. Little details of this sort can save you a lot of time and effort.

(d) You will also need a book of the rudiments (or elements) of music. There are many, inexpensive ones available. Make sure that the one you buy contains all the key signatures, time signatures and note groupings, lengths of notes and rests, the most common ornaments (acciaccaturas, appoggiaturas, mordents, turns, trills and shakes), signs and abbreviations, and a fairly lengthy list of musical terms; information on phrasing and an outline of the more common musical forms can also be very helpful. Many books will contain other information, but for playing purposes the above list is a reasonable minimum. Descriptions of common chords can be of interest too, but if you are considering examinations in musical theory you will need a book which deals with intervals, elementary harmony, word setting, and any other aspects which the syllabus for the particular examination requires. Colleges which set the examinations usually produce books to cover their own syllabus, and you would be well advised to obtain one which is appropriate to the examinations which interest you.

Now let us get down to the actual learning process. We cannot hope to give a satisfactory performance of any piece of music unless we can play the right notes, or at least most of them, so this is where to start.

Studying the Score Away from the Keyboard

(a) The famous Hungarian concert pianist Andor Foldes advises students to read the score of a new piece away from the keyboard at least twice before attempting to play it. His reasoning is that a clearer mental picture of the music can be gained "without being distracted by the physical aspects of its playing". Some students might have difficulty in making sense of the music without actually hearing it. Even looking at it, however, can be a help in gaining some notion of the rhythms, the rise and fall of the melodies, and the "physical aspects of its playing".

(b) At the same time, divide up the new piece into manageable divisions. I use the word 'division' rather than 'phrase', or any other term used in musical analysis, because each one can vary from a few notes to a few phrases. The size of each will be governed by the difficulties it contains. Work seems more manageable if a point of rest is in sight. But the advantages are not only psychological. A high level of concentration can be more satisfactorily maintained if the time span is short. Coupled with this, it is easy to forget how a particular difficulty was overcome by moving on too soon. The objective, at this as at all stages, is to make as few errors as possible; the size and content of each division is therefore very important. Marking each of them on the copy acts as a reminder of the sensible working lengths already chosen. As the practising gets under way it might be necessary to alter their size, but the temptation to make them longer, particularly when the work seems to be easy, should be resisted.

(c) Resist also the temptation to try your piece through a few times before you begin serious work on it.

Starting Work at the Keyboard

Having settled on your divisions, the next step is to work out fingering patterns. The chapter on fingering will help you to do this. Always begin by considering the fingering patterns suggested on your copy. Where you are experiencing real difficulty, try some patterns of your own which you feel might be better suited to your hands. I stress the word *real* because a fingering pattern which you find awkward might eventually be the only sensible one – any alteration to it still landing you in *real* difficulty. If your new piece is long, it is not necessary at this stage to finger each of its divisions, but do remember to check that the fingerings have been worked out before starting to practise any particular division.

Where to start practising is a matter of personal choice. It is not always necessary to begin at the beginning. Tackling a difficult division first can have some advantages, as can starting with a division near the end of the piece and working back, division by division, towards the beginning. The chosen starting point depends on the types of difficulty which are encountered. Each piece of music needs to be treated differently; but wherever that starting point is, be sure you have already worked out the fingering patterns.

Begin to practise so slowly that matters of timing and rhythm are almost irrelevant. Your brain must always be directing your fingers accurately to the next note or chord. If it is very hard going, do no more than a bar, or even half a bar, at a time, but make sure that you get it right and then take a short break. Practise both hands together as far as possible, because the decision-making process in playing will need to be programmed to use both hands together – using hands separately is an entirely different experience. If there are any particular movements from note to note or chord to chord giving real trouble, isolate them and practise hands separately, but revert to hands together as soon as possible. Carrying on too long with this type of intensive practice can result in loss of concentration and errors can creep in; continued work can create more problems than solutions. Taking short breaks, or putting in some work of a different nature on the previously well rehearsed piece, can be helpful in sustaining concentration. It is still necessary, however, to give as much time as possible to the problems of the chosen section of your new work until they have been mastered. It is so easy to forget the minute details of movement from note to note and chord to chord which a safe and satisfactory performance requires if you attempt to move on too soon.

Continue learning these details until the whole division can be played slowly, very firmly (i.e. about *f* at least, irrespective of the dynamic markings), and without inaccuracies or hesitations. Any slight feelings of doubt about what is coming next should be viewed with concern – they are mistakes waiting to be made. Try also to commit the section to memory, although it should not generally be played that way in case note errors creep in. Playing it, or parts of it, with eyes shut, or without putting the lights on, can help to concentrate thought on the notes themselves rather than on the printed copy. Continue practising slowly in this way until the division feels quite safe. Many repetitions will be needed, but keep concentrating all the time; do not give over to automation too soon.

Now select your next division and do likewise, making sure that everything is dealt with slowly and accurately. Never be tempted to skimp: you will pay for it later if you do. Work through division by division in the same painstaking way. Do not start at the beginning of the piece each time or you will know the opening much better than the rest of it. This might appear to be a long, slow way of learning, but in fact you will learn to play your piece accurately and confidently much more quickly than if you keep running through it at speed, making numerous errors on the way.

The Right Timing and Rhythm

Working with a Metronome

While the note learning process is continuing, begin to establish the correct timing and rhythms in the division where you have already learned the notes. Practise with a metronome. For many students this can be a frustrating and irksome stage, because playing in strict time to a metronome is not a particularly 'musical' occupation. At first you might feel like throwing the metronome out of the window, or cursing the manufacturer for making such an inaccurate machine. But keep trying – it is surprising how, with use, your metronome will begin to keep in time with you. Set the metronome at a very slow speed initially, and persevere until you can play exactly in time with it. A metronome with a bell or other device to mark the first beat in the bar can be helpful. Shaping the phrases, considerations of rubato and the like will come later; it is no use altering the tread of a beat until you know exactly where that beat is. In matters of phrase shaping and rubato, it is necessary to have something solid to deviate from and return to when embarking on the later stages of practice.

Honour the note lengths in all the parts, work carefully through each division and make sure that the timing and rhythms are secure, just as you did with the notes. This stage is in fact a way of consolidating the note learning. If fitting the notes into the correct rhythmic patterns causes any difficulties of fingering or any awkwardness in hand or arm movements, make the necessary re-adjustments immediately, altering details of fingering or methods of moving from note to note, and marking any such alterations on the score so that you do not forget. Keep the speed slow, and do not be anxious to get on with more musical aspects at the expense of notes and rhythms. When using your metronome, practise only short sections at any one time. The object is to get the note lengths and rhythms correct, not to produce a stilted and mechanical performance. Once the note lengths and rhythms of your short section are correct, dispense with the aid of the metronome, and play the section again in a more relaxed and flowing manner.

These two stages – right notes and right timing – are crucial to final success. Separating note-finding from rhythm and timing difficulties, and doing so at a very slow playing speed will greatly reduce the risk of errors. Mistakes are the last things you need at this sensitive stage in the learning process.

Studying Details of the Score at the Keyboard

Still in pursuit of an accurate early reading of your new piece, working on the right notes, the right timing, and the right rhythms should be coupled with a further close study of the score, this time at the keyboard instead of away from it. Always have a book of the rudiments of music handy to ensure that you understand all the signs and terms given on the score.

(a) Note Lengths

Make sure that you give each note its correct time value. This may seem so obvious as to be unworthy of mention, but it is surprising how frequently the sound of a piece can be transformed by taking care to play exactly the note lengths the composer wants. Look out particularly for notes which are to be held. For instance, a bass semibreve should be given its full four beats no matter what difficulties you encounter in playing the notes above it, even if you have to alter your fingering patterns to do so. Do not play it and then release it after about one beat because you are concentrating on the moving notes in the other parts. This advice applies to all note lengths – whatever the note values in the score, *honour them.* Don't forget that holding a note too long is as bad as not holding it long enough. This too is something that can happen when you are concentrating on many things at once. For safety's sake you can find yourself holding on to two or three notes when you should only be holding one. Releasing notes too soon, or holding them too long affects the texture of the music, making it either thinner or thicker than the composer intended. It also affects the harmonies. Be severe with yourself, check such details carefully and often – you might find that it makes the piece easier to play, particularly if you are holding down too many notes and as a consequence giving yourself unnecessary fingering problems.

(b) Dynamic Markings

Practice needs to be quite loud at first to ensure that all the notes are firm and that any mistake is noticeable, but, as time goes on, you should begin to alter the dynamics in accordance with the markings on your copy. Your rudiments book will give you the meaning of general dynamic markings and terms, but the problem then is, how loud is loud (*f*) or how soft is soft (*p*) and so on. To give yourself some guide, look through the complete piece and check the extremes of dynamic given. It is no use making an *mp* marking as soft as you can play, only to find that on the next page you are expected to play a passage *p*, and then later on another one *pp*. Look out for the *mf*, *f*, and *ff* markings too, and adjust your playing to accommodate.

Honour *crescendo* and *diminuendo* markings too, but remember that they mean 'getting louder' or 'getting softer' *gradually*: do not alter the dynamic immediately you see one of these instructions unless it is accompanied by the word *subito* (suddenly).

(c) Accents etc.

Alongside general dynamic markings, watch out for accent marks and tenuto marks. Your book of rudiments will show you the difference between the two. An accent mark is a little right-facing arrowhead placed above or below a note, and is an indication that you play this note louder than its neighbours. The actual loudness of any accented note depends on the context in which it appears; an accented note in a passage marked *f* will be louder than one in a passage marked *p*. There might also be *sf* (*sforzando*) markings which require the note or chord to which they refer to be strongly accented. Any individual accents such as these must never sound incongruous, they must be carefully judged and sensitively honoured to bring out the sense of the music.

A *tenuto* mark (a short, thick, black line above or below a note) is often wrongly interpreted simply as an accent. The word *tenuto* actually means 'held', which means that the note to which it applies should be held for at least its full length, or perhaps a little longer.

Staccato, staccatissimo (see pages 69 and 70), accent, tenuto and pause marks (in that order). Make sure that you understand exactly what the signs and terms on your score mean.

Although sustaining it, deliberately, in this way will give that note prominence, it should not be the same as accenting it.

Another indication to accent notes is *marcato*. When this word appears on the score, every note affected by it should be made prominent.

(d) Speed Variations

These will be shown in the list of terms in your rudiments book, but the following guidance might be helpful. Temporary variations in speed are called for on many occasions. *Rall* (*rallentando*) and *ritard* (*ritardando*) mean gradually slowing down, but *rit* (*ritenuto*) means hold back immediately. It is easy to confuse these instructions, they are different from each other and care is needed to read them correctly.

Although not strictly speaking a speed variation, the pause mark should be mentioned at this point. It applies only to the note over which it is placed, and its length is governed by the character of the music. It sometimes is accompanied by the word *lunga*, meaning long.

(e) Other Terms

Many other terms governing expression appear on musical scores. Frequently they are in Italian, but indications in French, German, and English are also used. Your rudiments book will list the most usual ones, but if you require more, there are inexpensive books available which will give you many more terms and abbreviations. Look up any unfamiliar term immediately: it is dangerous to make a guess. *Morendo*, for example, means 'less endo', it is an indication that the sound should die away.

Ornaments

There are other technical matters which should be carefully considered at this early stage too. The performance and interpretation of ornaments is one which frequently causes concern to aspiring pianists, sometimes even resulting in works which contain ornaments being avoided completely. The very word seems to strike terror into the hearts of many aspiring pianists. What notes should be played? How should they be played? How fast should they be played? How loud should they be? These are a few of the questions which are asked about ornaments, as well as the all embracing one of why should they be there in the first place?

Their purpose is to beautify the music, to make it more effective, or to show the technical ability of the performer. All too often the demonstration of technical ability is taken as the most important factor, resulting in scrambled notes and unsteady rhythm. It is better to relegate this aspect to a more subordinate position and concentrate on making the music more beautiful and effective.

Comfort can be taken from the view expressed by the famous pianist Rubenstein that "there are not today two musicians of the same opinion in regard to the reading of embellishments." To strive for the correct way to play any ornament is therefore a fruitless task if among accomplished musicians there are many views on how ornaments should be played, and, to some extent, on what notes they should contain.

As with all aspects of piano playing, however, the right notes must come first, before anything musically "beautiful and effective" can be done. To find some authoritative statement of what the right notes should be you can consult your rudiments book, but many good editions of music give realisations of ornaments too. This is where to start: the worst possible thing to do is to have a "tilt" at the ornament as you are reading through the piece. If you do, the rough and ready approximation you make is likely to be with you for a long time, making it difficult to establish an accurate rendering. The precise details of different types of ornamentation are beyond the scope of this book; however, many good guides to ornamentation are available.

Having established what notes you wish to play, isolate the ornament and practise it out of context before you consider trying to put it in place in the music. Play the notes slowly and firmly, in precisely the way they are written out in whatever source you are using. Pay particular attention to the finger needed to start the ornament and the finger on which you will finish it. It is important to get these right because the notes immediately preceding the ornament must lead you smoothly into it and the ending must run smoothly into the notes which follow it in the context of the music. These comments might seem to be unnecessary, but surprisingly they are often not considered early enough during preparation. If the ornament is to be practised out of context while the general work of learning the piece is to be continued, it is essential to know the fingering pattern which will lead into the ornament and that which will follow immediately after the ornament, just as it is when practising any other difficult passage out of context. Attention to these details will avoid the common mistakes of trying to begin an ornament from an almost impossible position and tumbling out of it into an equally impossible one. It is usually the fingering needed to play the ornament accurately which determines the preceding and subsequent fingering patterns. I make no apology for stressing this most strongly. To make doubly sure that you get it right, mark the fingering boldly on your copy, and stick to it.

Still out of context, continue practising the notes of the ornament slowly, deliberately, firmly, and loudly until they become automatic. When they are absolutely secure, begin to put the ornament into context. The first stage in doing so is to make sure that you land naturally on the first note of the ornament using the right finger. Practise doing this, and also give yourself sufficient thinking time as you approach it so you know exactly how you are going to play the ornament. When you have practised approaching with a clear mental picture of what is going to happen next, begin to incorporate the ornament into the context of the music, but do so regardless of the speed you have been practising the rest of the piece; make sure that you play the ornament no faster than you have been practising it out of context. Don't worry about the speeds being different. Just make sure that you go into the ornament on the correct finger and with a clear mental pre-perception of how you are going to play it; then actually play it at the slow practice speed, and go out from it into the context of the piece. Do this frequently until you are absolutely sure of what you are doing and that nothing happens which is not exactly under your control. This process will leave you with an ornament which, although correctly played, is out of time with the rest of music, but it is only when you are sure of the ornament that you can begin to increase the speed to match it into context.

As the speed increases, make sure that you are still playing the notes of the ornament clearly, cleanly, and in the right rhythm. Because many ornaments require you to replay the same note you must pick up your fingers. Much of the trouble in playing ornaments at speed occurs because a finger you wish to use again has not been raised properly and is, in fact, still holding down the note you wish to play again.

Even when you have successfully overcome the difficulties of the ornament, continue rehearsing it slowly out of context just to remind yourself of all the little actions which are needed.

As with other pieces of advice, it takes much longer to explain the process than it does to carry it out. Do not be tempted to cut corners in this or any other element you are practising. I have, on many occasions, narrowly escaped having my front bumper removed by other road users who were cutting corners. The results in your piano practice might not be so spectacular as they are on the road, but they could, musically, be just as dangerous.

Irregular Note Groupings

The use of irregular note groupings is another form of ornamentation. The usual ways of grouping notes are in pairs, or multiples of pairs (4s, 6s, 8s, and so on), or in threes (triplets) or multiples of threes (6s, 9s ,12s, and so on). In each of these groupings it is possible to structure our thinking into one pair, two pairs, three pairs, and so on, or one triplet, two triplets, three triplets, and so on.

The problem arises when notes are in patterns of five, seven, eleven or more notes and when grouping them into pairs or triplets would disturb the rhythmic flow. For instance, it is easy to think of a crotchet beat being broken down into two quavers, or a triplet group into three quavers. It is no more difficult to break such a beat down into four semiquavers, or even a pair of triplets, because in these cases we are breaking down the crotchet beat into regular sized groups, and to learn how to do so we can put a small emphasis on the first note of each group. What we then feel is that the number of notes within the space of a crotchet beat is increasing, and that because we can easily think in groups of twos or threes we can keep everything under control, provided the speed does not become too great.

Thinking in groups of five is less easy. Try the following exercise now. Set your metronome to 60 and count along with it:

(a)   **1 2 3 4**

Next, break this beat into pairs like this:

(b)   **1** 2 **2** 2 **3** 2 **4** 2

Keep the numbers in bold type exactly in time with the metronome beat and make them slightly louder than the small numbers between them.

Try the same exercise in threes like this:

(c)   **1** 2 3 **2** 2 3 **3** 2 3 **4** 2 3

Again keep the numbers in bold type strong and exactly in time with the metronome and make the small numbers weaker but fitting exactly. It is slightly more difficult at first to make everything coincide.

Try the same exercise in fives like this:

(d)   **1** 2 3 4 5 **2** 2 3 4 5 **3** 2 3 4 5 **4** 2 3 4 5

Now try the same exercise at the piano. Starting just with single notes as at (a) above, play a note C to each of the numbers in bold just to get used to the spacing. Next, counting in pairs as at (b) above, play that note C on the metronome beat and a note D on the small figures between each metronome beat. Next, counting in threes as at (c) above, play the notes C, D, E in triplets in the same way, and be aware of the difference in speed of the notes you are playing, even though the metronome beat remains constant. Again, the note C always comes on a metronome beat. Finally, counting in fives as at (d) above, play the notes C, D, E, F, G making sure that the note C always comes on a metronome beat, and be aware of the great increase in speed of the notes you are playing, even though you know the metronome speed is remaining constant. The aim in all cases is to begin each beat with the note

C exactly in time with the metronome. It takes concentration and careful listening to identify, and to be sure of getting rid of, all inequalities. You will notice that I have not used an & between any of the notes. This is the usual way of counting, but it is only appropriate when counting in pairs of notes. Counting triplets as 1 & & 2 & & and so on would be confusing, and it would become even more so if the number of &'s had to increase.

Other groupings beyond 5s can be practised similarly by increasing the number of counts between bold numbers and again using a metronome to keep the pulse steady. Fortunately, the greater the number of notes required in any group, the more latitude there is, aesthetically, for slight adjustments in speed. Such groupings are ornamentations to the musical line in just the same way as set piece ornaments and they often appear in even quite simple pieces of music. Like ornaments, they must be practised slowly until every note is secure. Fingering patterns should be carefully worked out so that evenness can be maintained.

Groups containing large numbers of notes usually require some form of special treatment. They could run to a climactic point and then come away from it within the space of the group; they could be played very softly and lightly; when carefully rehearsed, they might be played very quickly; they might be played very smoothly; or they might be played with a well controlled staccato. There are many possibilities, but the point I am making is that they must have a character suitable to the context in which they appear. There is often an instruction from the composer or editor to help you, but in the absence of any such instruction it is up to the performer to make sure that they enhance rather than encumber the musical line. Simply to rush at them because you see a lot of notes is certainly not the musician's answer.

Building an Aural Image

So far, discussion has centred on the note learning stage. Only when this work is secure can you safely begin to build up an interpretation of your chosen piece. Trying to come to terms with your impression of what the composer intended is the final stage of your work. As a first step to achieving this, it is necessary to create in your mind a clear aural image of how you want the music to sound. Further progress then depends on your emotional response to the music and how well you can convert your feelings into a musical entity, using whatever technical and musical elements you have learned. Your approach cannot be haphazard. To create an aural image you must listen to a great deal of music. Listening is an active pursuit and requires a detailed knowledge of exactly what you should be listening for. Casual, ill disciplined, and undirected listening can be as misleading and unhelpful as misdirected practice, and can lead you into errors of thought and action. Although it is in the final preparation for performance that a real understanding of the music reveals itself, the processes required to arrive at that level of understanding begin before any notes are struck and continue throughout the whole learning process. Active and concentrated listening is a skill which can be learned, but like any other it needs to be honed to perfection over a long period of time.

Background Reading

To begin learning this skill, some background reading can assist. It can bring you into direct contact with great artists and composers in a different way from listening to performances, and can give you words and ideas to help you to make constructive criticisms of your own performance. To be useful to you, these words and ideas must be as precise as possible. Vague exhortations and general references to impressionism, romanticism, and the like are at best only marginally helpful and at worst can make you believe you know more that you actually do. References should be as close to the source of the music as you can get. Actual descriptions and instructions by composers are best, but information from students who have worked with a composer or artist are a good second best. It is possible to find information of this sort in a variety of sources. Mozart's letters, for instance, contain first hand references from Mozart himself about his and other people's piano playing.

Information from such sources is always directly useful, even though it often needs to be carefully studied before it becomes so. Two similar views on the use of rubato, for instance, were given by Mozart and Chopin. Mozart wrote in a letter to his father from Augsburg, "What these folks cannot grasp is that in tempo rubato during an adagio the left hand should continue in strict time". Chopin's advice to his students about playing rubato was that, "The left hand is the conductor of the orchestra". Though expressing a similar idea, these statements are not identical. The conductor of an orchestra, whilst keeping a strict hold on speed and timing, does not necessarily keep strict time. Mozart's comment certainly does suggest strict time, but Chopin's advice could mean that the left hand was a restraining influence on a more exuberant right hand rather than it being an inflexible metronomic time keeper. It is this sort of information that can be much more to the point when you are trying to build an aural image of the music than are stories about a composer's love life, however interesting and colourful the latter might be.

Although of considerable interest to pianists, the general summaries contained in musical histories, in books on musical styles and in those dealing with particular historical periods, biographies of composers, and assessments of works, all need to be translated into practical terms before they can be of real use in creating a workable aural image of the music concerned. If we are not careful we can easily be lulled into thinking that we know how to interpret music of the classical, or some other period, simply by reading these generalisations.

We must sift through whatever books we can find very carefully, extracting any pieces of concrete information about methods of performance, and any direct references to the intentions of composers. Books written by, or about, famous pianists can also be helpful. What we must always be looking for is hard fact and specific information on how to do things, rather than opinions, psuedo-psychological examination, and the like.

Beware of writings that lead along paths which, in fact, bear little or no relation to the actual words or intentions of composers. A friend of mine, an eminent author, becomes very irritated when he reads comments about his intentions, or analyses of his style, which are ill informed, show lack of understanding, and often are actually wrong. For this reason he takes care to prevent early typescripts, or revisions of his work, becoming available to anyone who might begin speculating about underlying significances which do not, in fact, exist. Composers, especially those who are also well known performers, frequently suffer from this type of treatment. Since it is impossible in live performances to give identical renderings, many variants of interpretation, and even of notes, can eventually creep into the printed copies of their music. Such variants form grist for the mills of many writers who see significance in everything, provided it is done by someone famous.

Ian Wallace, the well known bass singer, tells a lovely story which illustrates this. At one point in a Benjamin Britten opera he had to climb up onto a table and hang something from a nail high up on a wall. During one particular performance he climbed up slowly and methodically as usual but found that some practical joker had removed the nail. He carefully climbed down again, making the action seem as much a part of the choreography as he could. In a review of that performance one critic made special reference to the symbolism and significance of this action. It behoves us to be careful. Good modern editions give reasons for, and comments about, variants, so careful reading of the well documented introductions to these can be both revealing and helpful.

The Architecture of the Music

Understanding the architecture of any piece of music, however simple, allows us to build to its climactic points wherever they might be, as well as to follow the progress of the important elements of the music, and show how they relate to each other. In a work of literature, the words themselves have meaning, enabling them to be phrased into sensible patterns, as was demonstrated earlier in the stanza from Tennyson. Music notes do not, in themselves, have any precise meaning, and even when they are grouped into phrases and short melodies their meaning is not, in the same sense, specific.

In performance, music only exists from moment to moment. It is possible to view a picture in total or in part. We can move our attention from element to element within it and relate this information again to the picture as a whole until we have understood its balance and perspective. In music, all has to be made clear as we proceed, there are no chances to look back or forward. Any review of material must be built into the musical shape, and the resultant form must be immediately intelligible. Unless it is so, music would be as the American writer Elbert Hubbard described life, "just one damn thing after another". Having understood the shape of a piece, we must use our skills to highlight what is essential at any particular moment, and bring it to the attention of listeners.

The important words at the beginning of the previous sentence are 'having understood the shape of a piece'. By reading and studying (not necessarily the same things) we can learn how to analyse the music we are intending to play. To make musical sense, certain elements must recur to compensate for our inability to look back and remind ourselves of them; we must therefore ensure that their reappearances are not just tedious repetitions. It is the ability to present them as new and interesting on their first appearance, as thought provoking acquaintances when they appear again later, and finally as well established old friends taking their temporary leave of us at the end, which matters.

There are other lines of enquiry to pursue as well. When a composer has given a name to a piece we have an immediate indicator for interpretative purposes. Some names, such as waltz, need little or no explanation, although checking the history of the waltz will reveal how the dance has changed over a period of time. The mood and character of other pieces become equally obvious when we know that their titles have a specific meaning. The titles *berceuse* (cradle song), *barcarolle* (boating song), *scherzo* (joke) tell their own story, and the performance of many other pieces, such as *toccatas* ('touch' or display pieces), *nocturnes* (literally 'night' pieces) and *fantasies* (pieces built on changing moods or fancies) can benefit from an explanation of their title. The musical dictionaries are sources from which to extract information. This line of approach might seem almost too obvious to be worth mentioning, but it is surprising how often it is neglected.

What is less obvious is that checking up on given names can be of assistance with pieces which are unnamed. Once you have become familiar with the features of a *gavotte* (a dance in four time in which the rhythm runs from the middle of each bar instead of from the beginning) or a *saraband* (a slow dance in three time with an emphasis on the second beat in the bar), or the gentle rhythm of a *siciliano* (a rustic dance in six-eight time) for instance, it is surprising how many untitled pieces display these features or rhythms, giving you an instant indication of how to play them. Much more could be written on these topics, but I hope that there is sufficient encouragement here to send you to books which do not purport to help with piano technique or perform-ance, but yet can be helpful in building that aural image which will guide your brain and hand in bringing to life under your fingers the music you wish to play.

Listening

Above all, purposeful listening is the best way of build-ing an aural image; casual listening of the 'let it wash over me' type will not do. An excellent performance can beguile. Good resolutions about concentrating on the interpretation and listening intently can quickly be forgotten when enjoyment takes over. A conscientious mature student once complained to me that he did not enjoy the way he was playing a particular piece. I startled him by pointing out that it was not his job to enjoy it. His job was the moment by moment control of phrasing, articulation, dynamics, speed, pedalling, and the many other skills which performing demands. What he was doing was attempting to combine the leisurely pursuit of enjoyment with the concentrated effort of performing; inevitably the music suffered and, being a musical person, he realised something was wrong. Enjoyment should not have been his goal at that moment. The satisfaction of almost achieving his aural image of the music (no one ever actually achieves it) by concentration and control was, however, within his grasp. He understood, and often reminded me of my comment, saying that it had focused his thoughts on the job in hand on numerous subsequent occasions.

The worst possible result of hearing an enjoyable performance given by a competent pianist is to suc-comb to the temptation of copying it. It is important to be aware of this hidden danger. That performance would have been born of a considerable amount of reading and listening on the part of the performer, as well as many hours of slow, painstaking practice at the keyboard. Slavishly copying it, however tempting the idea might be, cannot capture the thought, understanding, and effort which went into producing it. Without them the copy can never give satisfaction; the essential spark, created by study, would be missing. Your own spark, carefully ignited, might never burn as brightly as that of the performer you heard, but at least, if you listen to good purpose, it can be fanned into living flame rather than remaining some sullenly smouldering ember.

So much for the 'pep' talk; what actually needs to be done? You require a cassette, or CD, player, on which you can repeat a few bars of music. The recording should be as good as you can get, and it should be played on an amplification system which will give you as wide a range of frequencies as possible. If the high frequencies are missing, the starting transient of the notes will not be crisp and clear, and the general tone, although quite fulsome, will not be incisive; a woolly sound will tend to cover up some of the details of quality for which you must be listening. (Incidentally, my harpsichord was made by Dennis Woolley, an eminent English harpsichord and fortepiano maker. Mine is an early model and bears the name Köchel on its name board. Until he became well established he used this name, because, he asked, "Who would want to buy a woolly harpsichord?")

As well as good sound equipment, ideally you will need a score of the music you are listening to. If it is a work you are studying, obviously you will have a score;

but although not absolutely essential purely for listening purposes, it is highly desirable. You also need, of course, at least one recording of the work you wish to listen to. If you can get more than one, so much the better because interpretations differ. If you have only one recording there is still much you can learn from it without directly trying to copy it, but if you can compare one performance with another you can learn much more. Do not eschew your own recording. If your own performance of the work, or parts of it, is bearable, record it and listen to it. What you are trying to develop is a constructive critical approach to your listening, and you can be as analytical of a less accomplished performance as you can of an excellent one. Your criticism of a less accomplished performance might even offer you more scope for constructive comment.

Below, I have collected together many points to listen for. It is not presented as an exhaustive list, nor is it intended as one you will use while listening and tick off items as you go. Its purpose is to direct your thoughts, and your attention, to the types of detail which will help you when creating, and putting into practice, your own aural image. As your critical ability develops, you will be able to refine some of the suggestions, and add to them, but at least they will form a sound (please excuse the unintentional pun) basis for you to work on. I have presented my comments under separate headings in the hope that this will focus your attention on certain important areas.

Right Notes

If you have more than one copy, or more than one recording, you might come across some discrepancies in notes. The edition you are using should have some reference to any usual variants in the notation together with some explanation of why such variants exist.

If the work is one you are studying, you might find that you have made a few misreadings in notes. It is surprising how often a wrong note can creep into your playing. You might have begun by reading it wrongly, or you might initially have read it correctly and the error has, over a period of time, crept in and become so familiar to you that the correct note is disconcerting. This is one of the more mechanical and prosaic uses of listening to a recording, but it can be useful as well as revealing.

Ornaments

Ornaments have been discussed under a separate heading where it was made clear that there is much variation in the way they can be treated. Listening to a professional pianist can help in many ways, although what you hear should not be accepted as the one and only 'correct' interpretation.

Where the ornaments appear in your recording might not agree with their position in your score. An authoritative modern edition of the music could give reasons for this. Even if they are in the same position, the ornaments themselves might not be the same as those in your score. All that you can safely gather is that an ornament of the type, and in the position it is played, is acceptable. You then have to decide, from the information you have, what you prefer.

More important is to listen to how the ornaments are played. Listen for their precise position. Are they on, before, or after the beat? How many repetitions are there in the trills? How are the beginnings and endings of the ornaments treated? Do they start on an upper note, or the written note? Do they end with a turn? If not, how do they end? At what speed are they played? This is the sort of information which can be of real assistance to you in forming your aural image, but you may need to listen to any particular ornament many times before you can unravel such small details, particularly when they are played at speed.

Important Melodic or Harmonic Elements

Listen to how the performer directs attention to the important melodies; not only the main ones, but also subsidiary melodies, counter melodies, and even just a few notes which occasionally assume a fleeting importance. Sometimes the score does not show these subsidiary elements clearly. If this is so, it would do no harm to make reference to them on your score, whether or not you intend to use them.

If you have more than one recording, it is interesting to note what elements the artists consider important, and not only that, take note of how each of them makes you aware of what he feels is important. Does he do it by volume, emphasising the element, or subduing the less important one? Is it done by phrasing? Is it done by variations in the types of touch? Is it done by rubato? If none of these, how is it done?

Highlighting

Methods of highlighting have already been described. When an element is treated in this way some preparation is needed to match it with what has gone before and what follows. It might need careful listening on a few occasions to establish exactly how this is achieved. Your first impression might not actually be the correct one and a few repetitions might be needed to establish exactly what is happening. As well as listening to what was highlighted, check exactly what was subdued. Listen also to the few notes immediately preceding and following the highlighting to hear how it is matched in. Try to detect any alterations in speed, however slight. Are the notes spaced out a little more? Is there any general alteration in volume immediately before or after the highlighting? If so, was it sudden or gradual? These are the details you need to listen for.

Phrasing

There has already been some discussion of phrasing in Chapter 7. Bearing in mind what was mentioned then, work out how the pianist makes you aware of the phrasing; volume, tone quality, and breaks in continuity are among the many possibilities, as is any combination of these.

Listen to the shaping of the phrases, how they move towards, and away from, the climactic points. Since each phrase will end with some form of cadence, how is the finality, or lack of it, made obvious?

There needs to be balance in phrasing. Although the phrases themselves, their relative importance and their lengths, are established by the composer, this must be passed on to the listener. How does the pianist achieve this? Again you will be thinking in terms of variation of volume, tone quality, and speed, either singly or in combination. Try to be as specific as possible, particularly about how the phrases are shaped, matched and contrasted.

Spacing and Placing

The techniques of spacing and placing notes used by professional pianists are worthy of close study. Spacing is frequently used in speech. Clarity and emphasis can be enhanced by carefully separating words, and slightly elongating the spaces between them. This gently highlights particular words without the need for increased volume. The same technique is used in music. When skilfully done, spacing gives the effect of a very discreet ritenuto (see page 129) without any apparent slowing down. You might need to listen intently to your recording at times, because the secret of its success is that, unless you know, it can be difficult to detect how the effect is being produced.

Placing is very similar, except that it usually affects only one note or chord (otherwise, of course, it would be spacing). The placed note or chord is played firmly, deliberately, and slightly late, although it need not be particularly loud. As with spacing, the intention, when placing, is to highlight; force is not always necessary. It is not possible to enumerate all likely places at which placing might occur, but one such place is the apex note of a phrase. Just as the keystone of an arch binds that arch together, so can a carefully placed apex note bind a musical phrase into a unity.

You will find many instances of thoughtfully spaced and placed notes. Listen for them and learn how to use the techniques naturally, and without ostentation or sentimentality.

Accent

Each piece of music is likely to have a time signature indicating 2, 3, 4, or more beats in a bar. How is this information passed on by the pianist without having a noticeable accent at the beginning of each bar chopping up the flow of the music? This has much to do with phrasing. Just as there are strong and weak phrases, are there detectably strong and weak bars? Waltz time can sometimes sound more like $\frac{6}{8}$ than $\frac{3}{4}$ when a strong bar is followed by a weak one, an effect which can help to disguise what might become monotonous repetition, while still preserving the general rhythm.

Rhythmic Drive

One thing which is immediately felt if you play with an accomplished musician is the rhythmic drive of the music. It is not just the beat or pulse which holds you – the constant forcing of this as in much 'pop' music can become tedious – it is the inevitability of the next point of climax or repose. Try to work out how this rhythmic grip is achieved and maintained without monotony. How much of this is connected with accent forcing you to take notice of the rhythm, or the lack of it making the phrase seem long and leading you on? It can be difficult to 'shape' the music rhythmically by slight alterations in speed without creating a feeling of rhythmic uncertainty and insecurity, or a feeling that the music is being hurried and is on the verge of running out of control. Exactly how is this 'shaping' achieved in the performance you are studying? Is there some slight 'steadying' of the drive when a climatic point is approached so that the point is not reached too soon?

Try to find out why the rhythm seems inevitable with-out being monotonous.

Rubato

Does the pianist's control of rubato on your recording closely resemble the method advocated by Mozart and Chopin? Does the left hand play strictly in time while the right hand indulges its fancy, or is the rhythm in both hands altered and an effect of continuity and time keeping instead achieved by an immediate return to the original speed? Does that return appear to be controlled and driven more by the left hand than the right, or is there a general feeling that both hands take an equal share in the return to the original speed? It might be any of these, and the method used might vary during the music according to circumstances. Can you detect exactly how it is done on each occasion?

Dynamics

Sympathetic control of dynamics is vital, not only for creating the mood of the music, but also for the formation of pianistic tone. Check the dynamics used in the performance on your recording – do they match those on your score? They might not, but this does not mean that the performer has got it wrong. Since dynamics can vary from edition to edition, there is no way of knowing whether it is the performer, or the editor of your score, who is achieving the composer's intentions. What can be profitable is to try to establish if the dynamic markings used are absolute or compara-tive, by which I mean is a *piano* or a *forte* marking always of exactly the same or of very similar intensity within the course of the piece, or are some *piano*s or *forte*s louder or softer than others? Performers must have the freedom to express the music as it appears to them, so the likelihood is that the intensity of similar dynamic markings within the course of any piece will vary. It is detail of this sort which is helpful if you are to learn from reputable pianists.

Architecture

The structural necessity of repetition in a musical composition has already been mentioned, along with the suggestion that these repetitions should be played in a fashion suitable to their position. The way important melodic and rhythmic features are presented on their initial appearance, and their treatment when they reappear later in the work, can reveal many of the secrets of good performance. Take notice of any variations of touch, tone, dynamics, or speed, however slight, which the performer uses, and bear them in mind when you are building an aural image of your piece. In particular, be aware of how any of the subtle changes enhance the mood of the music and make its musical shape more satisfactory. Building up tension towards a climax, inducing a calming effect when approaching the end of a section or the end of the piece, and many other effects can be achieved by the sensitive use of musical materials which are similar. Careful listening will help you to do likewise.

Speed

'Speed kills' has often been used as a warning to motorists. It would do well also as a warning to pianists. The speed at which many professional pianists play well-known works often encourages aspiring piano players to believe that high speeds are essential. Such speeds are only gained after many years of practice and are not always justified. I am sorry to say that I have heard performances on record marred by excessive speed. Little details have come and gone before their significance can be properly assimilated, much to the detriment of the music. I am not alone in my views on this. Speed can be exciting, but it can also produce renderings which, musically, are less than satisfactory. My criticism does not apply to all pianists. Claudio Arrau, for instance, is sometimes criticized for using tempos which are unusually slow (until you try to emulate them yourself!). But, by considering the character and shape of every phrase, he is able to convey the spirit, and excitement, of the music without putting pressure on the speed. "Bravo", say I, what better compliment could be paid to any musician than that he had considered the character and shape of every phrase. We would all do well to follow his example, and resist the desire to be one of the fastest pianists around. Mozart was not impressed by excessive speed, as a comment in his letters about Abt Vogler's playing of one of his (Mozart's) concertos shows: 'speed kills'; it is musicality which ultimately impresses.

Having built your aural image, use it. Start by reading the score of your piece and imagining yourself playing it. Try to feel what it will be like to accomplish the performance you are 'auralising', and to capture the actual sensations in your fingers of how you will play the notes. If it helps, use a hard surface of some sort to 'play' on. Do this for short sections of your piece at a time, and then transfer these to an actual keyboard. Be very critical of the sound you are making.

When you feel you can bear it, make a recording of your playing. Remember that you are not making a recording for sale, you are using it as an aid to learning. When listening to the recording (it need not be of the whole piece), apply to your own performance the same critical standards you applied to that of the professional pianists. Pick up every detail which does not accord with your aural image and find out why. Although this might sound like soul destroying work, it isn't. You can gain great satisfaction from tracking down, and rooting out, faults. But do not be surprised if, occasionally, your performance's departure from your aural image is an improvement. If you have done your work well, taken care over details, and, during your playing on the recording, have been able to let the music take you over, you might find that you have reached a greater understanding of the music than you thought possible. In short, you might find that, at least for some portions of your piece, you are actually giving a 'performance'. If so, you will feel that all your work has been worthwhile.

Questions

1   *Why is it preferable, when choosing a new piece, to have never tried to play it before?*

2   *If you have played it before, what must you be prepared for, and why?*

3   *Why, when learning a new piece is it advantageous to have a reasonably well known piece on hand also?*

4   *It can be helpful to have a pencil and rubber, and possibly a note book, available on the piano. Why?*

5   *What sort of information would you look for in a book of rudiments?*

You may find that you are actually giving a 'performance'.

6   *How can studying the score away from the keyboard be helpful?*
7   *Why should you divide your new piece into manageable sized divisions before you begin the learning process?*
8   *What temptations should you resist?*
9   *Having selected the divisions of your new piece, what is the next step?*

10   *Why is it always sensible to consider the fingering sug-gested on your score?*

11   *Should you ever alter the suggested fingerings?*

12   *Why should you begin to practise at a very slow speed?*

13   *Why, even at this early stage, should you aim to play the notes without hesitations and inaccuracies, and how would you set about doing this?*

14   *What are the advantages of separating note learning from timing and rhythms when you begin the learning process?*

15   *What procedures would you follow when you begin learning the right timing and rhythms?*

16   *What are the advantages, and disadvantages, of working with a metronome?*

17   *Why is a further close study of the score at the keyboard necessary to your early reading of the new piece?*

18   *How can your book of rudiments be helpful during this further close study?*

19   *Why is it very important at this early stage that you check the meaning of the terms you encounter on the score?*

20   *What initial steps should you take to prevent mistakes in playing ornaments?*

21   *Why is it important to see that the fingering is firmly established before you attempt to fit an ornament into the context of the piece?*

22   *Why should you take particular note of the fingering required for the first and the last notes of the ornament?*

23   *What bearing might this have on the fingering patterns leading up to, and those following, the ornament?*

24   *What are the advantages of practising the ornament slowly and firmly out of context?*

25   *How would you then fit the ornament into the context of the piece?*

26 *How can you train yourself to play irregular groupings of notes in time?*

27 *What is meant by the term 'aural image'?*

28 *What sort of information about composers can be directly helpful to building an aural image?*

29 *How can general histories:*
   (a) Be helpful;
   (b) Be misleading
   in assisting you to build an aural image?

30 *In what ways can a study of musical form or architecture be helpful for performance?*

31 *How can the names of compositions give us ideas about their performance, and also about the performance of other works?*

32 *What are the dangers of trying to copy a performance given by an eminent pianist?*

33 *What can be learned from listening to performances by eminent pianists?*

34 *How can you begin to teach yourself to listen critically and constructively?*

35 *What can listening critically and intently to your own performances and those of others help you to learn about the following aspects in performance:*
   (a) Ornaments and ornamentation;
   (b) Dealing with important melodic and harmonic elements;
   (c) Highlighting;
   (d) Building phrases;
   (e) Spacing and placing notes;
   (f) Accent and rhythmic drive;
   (g) Treatment of dynamics;
   (h) Form and architecture;
   (j) Sensible ways of using and controlling speed?

Index